COME, THOU
LONG-EXPECTED
JESUS

ADVENT AND CHRISTMAS
WITH CHARLES WESLEY

COME, THOU LONG-EXPECTED JESUS

ADVENT AND CHRISTMAS WITH CHARLES WESLEY

PAUL WESLEY CHILCOTE

MOREHOUSE PUBLISHING

AN IMPRINT OF CHURCH PUBLISHING INCORPORATED
HARRISBURG – NEW YORK

Unless otherwise noted, the Scripture quotations contained herein are from the New Revised Standard Version Bible, copyright © 1989 by the Division of Christian Education of the National Council of Churches of Christ in the U.S.A. Used by permission. All rights reserved.

Morehouse Publishing, 4775 Linglestown Road, Harrisburg, PA 17105

Morehouse Publishing, 445 Fifth Avenue, New York, NY 10016

Morehouse Publishing is an imprint of Church Publishing Incorporated.

Cover design by Laurie Klein Westhafer

Library of Congress Cataloging-in-Publication Data

Chilcote, Paul Wesley, 1954-
  Come, thou long-expected Jesus : Advent and Christmas with Charles Wesley / Paul Wesley Chilcote.
     p. cm.
  Includes index.
  ISBN 978-0-8192-2250-3 (pbk.)
  1. Advent—Meditations. 2. Christmas—Meditations. 3. Wesley, Charles, 1707–1788—Poetry. I. Title.
BV40.C465 2007
242'33—dc22
                          2007019188

Printed in the United States of America

07 08 09 10 11 12   10 9 8 7 6 5 4 3 2 1

CONTENTS

INTRODUCTION

Love divine, all loves excelling,
    Joy of heaven, to earth come down,
Fix in us thy humble dwelling,
    All thy faithful mercies crown!
Jesu, thou art all compassion,
    Pure, unbounded love thou art;
Visit us with thy salvation!
    Enter every trembling heart.
                            (*Hymns*, Hymn 374.1)

This well-known stanza from one of Charles Wesley's nine thousand hymns enunciates the central themes of his life and ministry. In Christ he encountered the pure, unbounded love of God, a love that transcends all others and defines our lives as the children of God. His image of God revolves around the Incarnation—the coming of God into human history in the person of Jesus Christ—and the mercy and compassion God extends to all people. The heart dominates his vision of Christianity because faith consists in relationships of love. God visits us in Jesus and offers us life abundant through the power of the Holy Spirit. The seasons of Advent and Christmas provide a unique opportunity to draw inspiration from this great theologian of the Anglican Communion.

The year 2007 marks the tercentenary of Charles Wesley's birth (December 18, 1707–March 29, 1788). Like his more well-known brother, John (1703–1791), Charles was an Anglican in earnest. As a devout priest of the Church of England, The Book of Common Prayer, the rhythms of Morning and Evening Prayer in the context of the liturgical year, and frequent participation in the Eucharist shaped his spirituality and understanding of the Christian faith. Charles Wesley's hymns remain a monumental devotional treasure of the Church of England. But they also expound the great themes of Christian theology. Most of the Anglicans who attached themselves to the Methodist movement learned their theology, in fact, through the hymns of this great poet theologian. Wesley's warm, evangelical faith and fervent, eucharistic spirituality shaped the Anglicanism of his day more than most realize, and his masterful hymns continue to shape global Christianity in our own time.

Can you imagine the seasons and great festivals of the Christian year without "Lo! He comes, with clouds descending," "Come, thou long-expected Jesus," "Hark! the herald angels sing," "Christ the Lord is risen today," "Hail the day that sees him rise," "Spirit of faith, come down"? How impoverished our worship would be without "Christ, whose glory fills the skies," "Rejoice, the Lord is King!" "O for a thousand tongues to sing," "Let the saints on earth in concert sing," "Ye servants of God, your Master proclaim," "Love divine, all loves excelling," and "Jesus, Lover of my soul." The father of the English hymn, Isaac Watts, claimed that one of Charles's hymns, "Come, O Thou Traveler Unknown," celebrating the "Pure, Universal Love of God," was worth all the hymns he himself had ever penned.

The purpose of this little devotional work is twofold. First, I hope that these Scripture readings, hymns, meditations, and prayers will help to prepare you for the coming of Christ anew into your life and enrich your observance of these seasons. Nothing would be more pleasing to Charles Wesley than open and trembling hearts more fully prepared to receive God's love after reflection on these devotional texts. Second, I seek to locate Wesley squarely in his Anglican heritage and to enable many outside (and within) the circle of Methodism to discover him as a profound mentor for faithful Christian discipleship. With regard to this second goal and to set the larger context for these readings, let me add a few more words about the spirituality of this great man of God and his appreciation for the season of reflection and celebration into which you are entering.

Charles Wesley's vision of the Christian life revolves around clear principles that have stood the test of time and resonate fully with his Anglican heritage. Among the salient themes of his spirituality are the foundation of grace, the centrality of accountable discipleship, including the connection between acts of piety and acts of mercy, the importance of Holy Communion, and the gift of song.

"Grace upon grace" summarizes Wesley's understanding of the Christian life. Discipleship begins in grace, grows in grace, and finds its ultimate completion in God's grace. Grace is God's unmerited love, restoring our relationship to God and renewing God's own image in our lives. Life, to put it simply, is all about a God who delights in relationships that liberate and restore the human spirit. Christian discipleship—the arena of God's continuing activity in the life of the believer—is, first and foremost, a grace-filled response to the free gift of God's all-sufficient grace.

> What shall I do my God to love?
> My loving God to praise
> The length, and breadth, and height to prove,
> And depth of sovereign grace?
>
> Thy sovereign grace to all extends,
> Immense and unconfined;
> From age to age it never ends;
> It reaches all mankind.
> (*Redemption Hymns*, Hymn 91.11–12)

Charles Wesley modeled accountable discipleship and developed structures that affirmed each Christian's need of others to successfully complete the journey of faith. He celebrated the spirit of the small groups in which the people called Methodists provided mutual encouragement and genuine care for one another.

> Help us to help each other, Lord,
> Each other's cross to bear;
> Let each his friendly aid afford,
> And feel his brother's care.

Help us to build each other up,
Our little stock improve;
Increase our faith, confirm our hope,
And perfect us in love.

(*Hymns*, Hymn 489.3–4)

Drinking deeply from the wells of his Anglican heritage, Wesley developed a comprehensive vision of theology and the Christian life characterized by an unusually wide embrace. He carefully balances personal salvation and social service, faith and works, heart and head, individual and corporate, Word and Table. He links "works of piety" with "works of mercy" to nurture and sustain growth in grace and love. Immersion in the means of grace and participation in acts of justice fueled the Wesleyan movement within Anglicanism and enabled it to become a powerful evangelical and eucharistic awakening.

Holy Communion anchored Charles Wesley's spirituality as a profound sign and act of God's offer of personal redemption and call to servant ministry. In one of his 166 *Hymns upon the Lord's Supper*, published in 1745, he bears witness to the priority of the Lord's Table among the means of grace:

The prayer, the fast, the word conveys,
When mix'd with faith, Thy life to me;
In all the channels of Thy grace
I still have fellowship with Thee:
But chiefly here my soul is fed
With fulness of immortal bread.

(*HLS*, Hymn 54.4)

Participation in this sacred meal elicits gratitude and thanksgiving as the keynotes of the Christian life and empowers the faithful to live in and for God's peaceable rule. Above all things, Wesley sought to share this good news with others and to express his gratitude through a eucharistic life.

Charles Wesley left behind his most important legacy in an amazing collection of hymns—his gift of song. If Augustine was right in making the claim that to sing is to pray twice, then Charles most certainly fulfilled St. Paul's injunction to pray without ceasing! Singing praise to God transforms the singer. Sacred song shapes the people of God. Charles Wesley's lyrical theology points to the centrality of grace, encourages accountable discipleship in such a way as to promote holiness of heart and life, and proclaims the ultimate foundation of all things in God's unconditional love for us all in Christ Jesus. The Wesleyan hymns help us rediscover our essential identity as children of God. They teach us how to integrate Christian faith and practice. They enable us to experience the inclusivity of the community of faith through the very act of singing together. Wesley's hymns continue to function as a powerful tool in God's work of spiritual transformation and renewal.

The seasons of Advent and Christmas afford a perfect opportunity to draw close to God through Jesus Christ and to ponder the mystery of the incarnation. The themes of this season impress upon the faithful follower of Christ the need to remain attentive, the expectancy of living in hope, the quest for peace in broken lives and a fragmented world, and the joy and wonder of God's love incarnate in Jesus Christ. The hymns of Charles Wesley frame this devotional manual for a spiritual pilgrimage through the forty days of this sacred period of the Christian year. Scripture readings appropriate for these seasons, and meditations and prayers that tie the themes of Word and hymn together afford a unique opportunity for you to plumb the depths of God's amazing love come down at Christmas.

"Come, thou long-expected Jesus" and "Hark, the herald angels sing," are widely known and sung around the world today. They hardly require introduction or explication. In 1745, however, in characteristic fashion, Charles Wesley published a collection of *Hymns for the Nativity of Our Lord*, specifically for use in the Christmas season. These eighteen sacred texts are a lyrical expression of Wesley's theology of the incarnation. All of these hymns are featured in this volume, as well as twenty-two additional hymns drawn from his wider poetic corpus. Most of the remaining hymns come from Wesley's *Collection of Hymns for the Use of the People Called Methodists* (1780), but selections are also featured here from his *Hymns and Sacred Poems* (1739, 1740, 1749), *Preacher Hymns* (1760), *Scripture Hymns* (1762), and *Family Hymns* (1767), as well as several recently published texts. The various hymn sources are cited at the end of this volume. Charles Wesley captures the wonder and majesty of the Advent and Christmas seasons in this amazing collection of hymns.

Advent prepares us for the coming of Christ. This season is like a gradual ascent up a mountain path, leading to a vision of unparalleled splendor. During this four-week period we examine ourselves and our lives. We prepare to receive the gift of Jesus. We contemplate this season, quieting our hearts and minds as we await God's self-revelation. The last season to be officially added to the church calendar, Advent now launches the church year, beginning the story of Jesus' life, death, and resurrection, and pointing to the consummation of all things in him. One of the great liturgical traditions associated with Advent is the recitation of the so-called "O Antiphons" during the final week of the season. Familiar to us because of the hymn "O come, O Come, Emmanuel," based on the antiphons, these prayers highlight seven titles attributed to Jesus. These antiphons, as well as Wesley's hymns, will frame our prayer in the final steps we take toward the great celebration of Jesus' birth.

Christmas, of course, celebrates the coming of God into this world in the person of Jesus of Nazareth. In Jesus, God manifests his loving nature; through the incarnation, God takes on the new name of Emmanuel—"God with us." The twelve-day season of Christmas radiates light, brings joy to the world, and heralds the glory of the God of love, but it also reflects realistically upon the call to Christian discipleship. The days following the great festival provide not only an opportunity for the faithful to reflect on the mystery of the incarnation, they actually constitute a mini-catechism for those who are learning about the faith. What a great opportunity to rediscover this ancient use of the "Twelve Days of Christmas"! We know about the "partridge in a pear tree," but the deeper spiritual meaning of these days is lost to most people. To illustrate, the third day represents the three theological virtues of faith, hope, and love. Rather than "five golden rings," the traditional reference is to the Torah, the first five books of the Bible. Seven symbolizes the gifts of the Holy Spirit in Romans 12; eight represents the Beatitudes of Matthew 5; ten—can you guess?—stands for the Ten Commandments. Not only can this catechetical tradition help you remember some of the basic Christian tenets, it can help you ponder the enduring significance of the incarnation and enrich your relationship with the God of love.

My invitation to you is simple. Come. Immerse yourself in these wonderful means of grace. Find yourself "lost in wonder, love, and praise!"

How to Use This Book

The season of Advent begins four Sundays prior to December 25. Since Christmas falls on a different day of the week each year, the fourth week of Advent, more often than not, is never really finished. Is this not a parable of life? The fact that Jesus' birth breaks in upon us in the midst of life surprises us with joy. The length of the Advent season, therefore, varies from year to year. The longest possible season is twenty-eight days; it may be as short as twenty-two days. This devotional manual includes readings for a full twenty-eight-day Advent season, which make up Part 1 of the book.

There are a number of ways you can use the materials in Part 1, given the different length of the Advent season from year to year. Perhaps the simplest thing to do is to begin at the beginning and, on Christmas day, switch to Part 2, which contains materials for the twelve days of Christmas. When the season of Advent is short, however, and requires that you skip readings during the final week of Advent that are of particular significance, I recommend that you double up the readings for Advent III and IV, using one reading in the morning and one in the evening. This will enable you to work through all of the material in sequence. Feel free to break the pattern, however, so as to fill the days leading up to and following Christmas with prayer and reflection. The resources are here for you to use as you see fit, and you may discover other creative ways to include all the readings. Given the stability of the twelve days of Christmas, your use of Part 2 is much more straightforward.

Each of the forty readings includes a biblical text, a Wesley hymn selection, a brief meditation, and a prayer for the day. The devotional exercise begins, appropriately, in the word of God. I have provided an index of Scripture sources I have cited, so that you can see the range of biblical material at a single glance. The hymns of Charles Wesley are arranged around traditional Advent and Christmas themes and keyed to the scriptural texts proper to each day. The name of a hymn tune recommended for singing the text, as well as the title of a standard hymn sung to the same meter, accompanies each hymn, if appropriate. These suggestions are drawn from *The Hymnal 1982* of the Episcopal Church, but the hymn tunes and meters can be located in the index of the standard hymnals of many traditions. The meters of the hymns and the suggested tunes are also collected in an index.

One of the issues I struggle with is Wesley's pervasive use of gender-specific language with reference to humanity in his hymns. This distinguishes his age from our own. I am strongly committed to the use of inclusive language in all my writing and teaching. My decision in the end, however, was to retain the original language of Wesley's poetry in order to maintain the historical integrity of these powerful texts. I pray that this does not prove to be an insurmountable barrier to the truth and wisdom of his words. Whenever you encounter masculine references, I invite you to break out of these gendered images; you may even want to attempt a new rendering of the text that retains the poetic form but is more sensitive to inclusivity.

Take time with the hymns. Meditate on them. Ponder the deep meaning of the words as they relate to the gift of Christ to the world and to you. The brief meditation and prayer provide a focus for reflection that, hopefully, will lead to action.

Part 3 of this book provides a pattern of either Morning or Evening Prayer into which you may insert these devotional materials as part of a longer liturgical observance. These formats are particularly suitable for corporate or parish prayer, group use, or a more developed individual plan of spiritual formation through these seasons. The purpose of these readings is to enrich your Advent and Christmas and to provide a means by which individuals, families, discipleship groups, parishes, and congregations may live and sing, "Glory to the newborn King!"

PART ONE

Hymns and Prayers for Advent

ADVENT I: WAITING IN HOPE

FIRST SUNDAY IN ADVENT

Read

> I wait for the LORD, my soul waits, and in his word I hope;
> my soul waits for the LORD more than those who watch for
> the morning, more than those who watch for the morning. O
> Israel, hope in the LORD! For with the LORD there is steadfast
> love, and with him is great power to redeem. It is he who will
> redeem Israel from all its iniquities. (Psalm 130:5–8)

Sing

Meter: 87.87

This hymn can be sung to Stuttgart, the traditional setting for this
hymn.

> Come, thou long-expected Jesus,
> Born to set thy people free,
> From our fears and sins release us,
> Let us find our rest in thee:

Israel's strength and consolation,
   Hope of all the earth thou art,
Dear desire of every nation,
   Joy of every longing heart.

Born thy people to deliver,
   Born a child and yet a King,
Born to reign in us for ever,
   Now thy gracious kingdom bring:

By thy own eternal Spirit,
   Rule in all our hearts alone,
By thy all-sufficient merit
   Raise us to thy glorious throne.
                    (*Nativity Hymns*, Hymn 10)

Reflect

In the season of Advent we explore the ways in which God comes to us. We reflect upon the manner of God's first coming into human history in the birth of Jesus. God comes to us in the present moment in ways that surprise, challenge, and inspire us. We confess that God will return to us again when we acclaim at the eucharistic feast, "Christ has died. Christ is risen. Christ will come again." This season reminds us that our God is a God who comes to those who wait.

Sometimes we yearn so much for God in our lives that the expectation is almost too much for us. Our needs press in upon us. The demands of life overwhelm us. We long for God in the midst of it all. We hope, sometimes it seems beyond hope, for an appearance, a sign, a word, a presence. The Israelites, God's own people, lived in that kind of collective expectation, and Charles Wesley attempted to capture their feelings—our feelings—in this familiar Advent hymn. God comes and brings liberation from fear and sin, offering rest and peace. However, God does not offer a historic event or a momentary release. God comes to reign in us forever, to rule our hearts, and to raise us up through the power of the Spirit.

As you begin this Advent journey, what is your deepest hope? Are you yearning for something in your life? Do you seek to know and love God, even as you are known and loved by Jesus? When God comes, how might God's advent change your life? What transformation accompanies the birth of Christ anew in your heart? Ask God to reign and rule in your life, and to raise you into a joyous life of grace and peace and hope. Come, thou long-expected Jesus!

Pray

   O Loving God, whose advent we celebrate throughout this journey of hope: Come, and renew our hearts and minds through the presence of the Spirit of Christ. Amen.

MONDAY IN ADVENT I

Read

   For once you were darkness, but now in the Lord you are light. Live as children of light—for the fruit of the light is found in all that is good and right and true. Try to find out what is pleasing to the Lord. Take no part in the unfruitful works of darkness, but instead expose them. For it is shameful even to mention what such people do secretly; but everything exposed by the light becomes visible, for everything that becomes visible is light. Therefore it says, "Sleeper, awake! Rise from the dead, and Christ will shine on you." (Ephesians 5:8–14)

Sing
Unusual Meter: 665 11

> O astonishing grace,
> That the reprobate race
> Should be reconciled!
> What a wonder of wonders that God is a child?

> The Creator of all,
> To repair our sad fall,
> From heaven stoops down:
> Lays hold of our nature and joins to his own.

Our Immanuel came,
The whole world to redeem,
And incarnated showed
That man may again be united to God!

And shall we not hope,
After God to wake up,
His nature to know?
His nature is sinless perfection below.

To his heavenly prize,
By faith let us rise,
To his image ascend,
Apprehended of God, let us God apprehend.

(*Nativity Hymns*, Hymn 14)

Reflect

Charles Wesley preached a valedictory sermon to the Oxford University community entitled "Awake, Thou that Sleepest" at famous St. Mary's Church in 1742. He admonished his hearers to awake from their lack of concern about spiritual needs, from satisfaction in their sin, from contentment in their brokenness, from arrogance and self-centered complacency. The sermon did not go over well, despite the fact that he encouraged the students to reclaim their true identity as God's children and to receive God's promise of light, liberation, and love to fill their lives. Charles lamented that so many seemed to prefer the darkness.

If we have eyes to see, however, aroused by the light of Christ, we wake to an astonishing grace. God does not wait for us to make the first move. Even as we sleep, the Spirit works in our lives to arouse us from our slumber. Countless acts of mercy, love, and grace surround us day in and day out. God attempts to get our attention in events, through the influence of other people, in sign-acts of love in the church. But most importantly, God wakes us up by coming to us in the person of Jesus Christ. Like the first light of dawn, the beams of this marvelous Light dance around us. The light breaks into the darkness of our sleep and awakens us to a new reality in our lives.

This Light reveals that you need no longer live as an alien from God. Rather, through Christ, God repairs your broken life and welcomes you back into a loving embrace. Not only that, as you participate in Christ—as you live in and for his way of love—God conforms you to the wholesome and life-giving image of Jesus. Known fully by God, you begin to know God, and you rise to take on the marvelous image of Christ.

Notice that the writer to the Ephesians does not say, "For once you were *in* darkness, and now you have seen the light." No, a much larger vision captured his imagination! Because of the incarnation of God in Christ, you have been given the awesome privilege and responsibility of *being* light in a dark world as you trust and hope in the Light of the world.

Pray

Great God of Light, arouse us from our sleep, shine your light upon us, and fill us with hope, so that your glorious light might shine through our lives as it did in Christ. Amen.

TUESDAY IN ADVENT I

Read

"Beware, keep alert; for you do not know when the time will come. It is like a man going on a journey, when he leaves home and puts his slaves in charge, each with his work, and commands the doorkeeper to be on the watch. Therefore, keep awake—for you do not know when the master of the house will come, in the evening, or at midnight, or at cockcrow, or at dawn, or else he may find you asleep when he comes suddenly. And what I say to you I say to all: Keep awake." (Mark 13:33–37)

Sing

Meter: CM
This hymn can be sung to Winchester Old, the tune used for "While Shepherds Watched Their Flocks."

I want a principle within
        Of jealous, godly fear,
A sensibility of sin,
        A pain to feel it near.

That I from thee no more may part,
        No more thy goodness grieve,
The filial awe, the fleshly heart,
        The tender conscience give.

Quick as the apple of an eye,
        O God, my conscience make;
Awake my soul when sin is nigh,
        And keep it still awake.

If to the right or left I stray,
        That moment, Lord, reprove,
And let me weep my life away
        For having grieved thy love.

O may the least omission pain
        My well-instructed soul,
And drive me to the blood again
        Which makes the wounded whole.

                                    (*Hymns*, Hymn 299)

Reflect

Once awakened to God's presence, it is important to remain alert to the obstacles and impediments to authentic life that surround you. When my family and I lived in Kenya, our African friends told us that we should never venture out into the night without a flashlight. Only on one occasion, early on, were we caught unawares. The African night quickly breaks in on you, dark as dark can be. If there is no moon to help illuminate your path, it is difficult to see even a few feet in front of your face. After explaining the difficulty we had that one evening even finding our way home—let alone avoiding the dangerous obstacles we encountered along the way—one of our dear Kikuyu friends said, "But

I told you to take a light. I know you have the light. Why did you not carry it into the darkness and stay alert?"

My mother possessed simple, but profound, wisdom with regard to spiritual matters. "I Want a Principle Within" was one of her favorite hymns. She told me often that it reminded her of her need to remain alert, to stay on the proper course, to rely on the indwelling Christ to maintain her bearings in life. An external guide is often helpful, even essential, on a journey. But nothing is more important than an internal guidance mechanism: a "principle within," an interior light that shines in your heart, keeps you alert, keeps you awake, so that you will avoid the danger of straying away from the narrow path of your journey.

Waiting in hope is not always as easy as we would like for it to be. The discipline carries us sometimes into dark places as much as it propels us toward the light. But this is a good thing. We need challenges in our life with Christ. As in the parable, God asks for us to remain vigilant. Christ has awakened your soul; it is now a part of your responsibility to "keep it still awake."

Pray

Surprising God, you arrive sometimes when and where we least expect you: Come, to sustain us in our waiting and to keep us ever vigilant in the watch. Amen.

WEDNESDAY IN ADVENT I

Read

The days are surely coming, says the LORD, when I will fulfill the promise I made to the house of Israel and the house of Judah. In those days and at that time I will cause a righteous Branch to spring up for David; and he shall execute justice and righteousness in the land. In those days Judah will be saved and Jerusalem will live in safety. And this is the name by which it will be called: "The LORD is our righteousness." (Jeremiah 33:14–16)

Sing

Meter: 77.77

This hymn can be sung to The Call, the tune used for "Come, my Way, my Truth, my Life."

> Come, Divine Immanuel come,
> Take possession of thy home;
> Now thy mercy's wings expand,
> Stretch throughout the happy land.
>
> Carry on thy victory,
> Spread thy rule from sea to sea;
> Re-convert the ransom'd race;
> Save us, save us, Lord, by grace.
>
> Ears to hear the Gospel sound,
> "Grace doth more than sin abound";
> God appeared, and man forgiven,
> Peace on earth, and joy in heaven.
>
> O that every soul might be
> Suddenly subdued to thee!
> O that all in thee might know
> Everlasting life below!
>
> Now thy mercy's wings expand,
> Stretch throughout the happy land,
> Take possession of thy home,
> Come, Divine Immanuel, come.
>
> (*HSP* [1749], v. 1, pp. 4–6)

Reflect

The people of Israel experienced and knew the hopelessness of bondage all too well. Oppressed by powerful military regimes, they abandoned any hope of restoration through human means. The prophets inspired them to put their trust in Yahweh and some form of divine intervention. They believed that God would restore the house of David through an anointed one—the Messiah—who would liberate them and establish the rule of God. Georg Friedrich Handel set this vision to flight in the music of his best-known work, *Messiah*. This amazing microcosm of Christian doctrine and faith became famous, not through its connection with the composer, but through its annual benefit performance at the Foundling Hospital for underprivileged children in London. This Christmas tradition reminded the poor of God's prophecy of salvation, the redemptive sacrifice of Christ, and the promise of the resurrection.

Charles Wesley's hymn prays for the extension of this rule in the hearts of everyone, everywhere. Enamored of the idea of flight and wings, Wesley exploits this image to describe the spread of righteousness and justice throughout the world. The wings of God's mercy expand, stretch out, carry on, and spread God's rule from sea to sea. Wings become buoyant on the wind of the Spirit that lifts us into the presence of God, who offers mercy and peace, righteousness and justice to all. The invitation to join in the flight extends to every person, and those who open their hearts to God's presence find themselves subdued by the power of hope and love. Notice how Charles inverts the first and the last stanzas of the hymn, returning to the image of mercy's wings and inviting the Messiah to come. Fly up to him who loves you so.

Pray

Merciful God, fulfill your promises anew in my life. Lift me up into your presence through the power of the Holy Spirit who is ever at work to make me whole. Amen.

Thursday in Advent I

Read

But this I call to mind, and therefore I have hope: The steadfast love of the Lord never ceases, his mercies never come to an end; they are new every morning; great is your faithfulness. "The Lord is my portion," says my soul, "therefore I will hope in him." The Lord is good to those who wait for him, to the soul that seeks him. It is good that one should wait quietly for the salvation of the LORD. (Lamentations 3:21–26)

Sing

Meter:10 10.11 11

This hymn can be sung to Hanover, the tune used for "O Worship the King."

All glory to God, And peace upon earth,
Be published abroad At Jesus's birth:
The forfeited favour Of heaven we find
Restored in the Saviour And Friend of mankind.

Then let us behold Messias the Lord,
By prophets foretold, By angels adored;
Our God's incarnation, With angels proclaim,
And publish salvation In Jesus's name.

Our newly-born King By faith we have seen,
And joyfully sing His goodness to men,
That all men may wonder At what we impart,
And thankfully ponder His love in their heart.

What moved the Most High, So greatly to stoop?
He comes from the sky Our souls to lift up;
That sinners forgiven Might sinless return
To God and to heaven, Their Maker is born.

Immanuel's love, Let sinners confess,
Who comes from above, To bring us his peace;
Let every believer His mercy adore,
And praise him for ever, When time is no more.
(*Nativity Hymns*, Hymn 7)

Reflect

Lamentations? The text for today hardly sounds like it would come from a book with such a title. The book opens with bitter weeping.

Treachery, suffering, servitude; uncleanness, shame, affliction; destruction, scorn, tribulation. These are the images that fill the opening chapters of this litany to defeat and desperation. Having catalogued the most incomprehensible set of circumstances imaginable and in the midst of "affliction and homelessness," the writer exclaims: "But this I call to mind." How is this calling to mind, reminding the reader of God's steadfast love, limitless mercies, and eternal faithfulness, even a possibility?

Northern and Southern Sudan have waged war against each other for thirty years. The more recent conflict in the Darfur region spawned genocide on the people of Western Sudan. Christians in Sudan have endured the widespread destruction of their churches, have been tortured for their faith, and have seen their priests and catechists crucified and burned alive. The suffering defies comprehension. But if you ask Sudanese brothers or sisters in Christ about the plight of their life, they respond fervently: "But this I call to mind. In the day of devastation, give thanks; and in the day of contentment, give thanks. Evil is departing and holiness is advancing. Evil has no power in the face of God's love. I will meditate on and talk of God's wonderful mercies! God has not forgotten us!"

Wesley proclaims the wonders of this glorious God made known to us through the incarnation. All people wonder at the witness of the faithful in a place like Sudan. They stand awestruck by what they impart, "And thankfully ponder His love in their heart."

Pray

Source of all truth and peace, we have hope because your steadfast love never ceases and your mercies never end; they are new every morning; great is your faithfulness. Amen.

Friday in Advent I

Read

I reprove and discipline those whom I love. Be earnest, therefore, and repent. Listen! I am standing at the door, knocking; if you hear my voice and open the door, I will come in to you and eat with you, and you with me. (Revelation 3:19–20)

Sing

Meter: 88.88.88

This hymn can be sung to St. Catherine, the tune used for "Faith of Our Fathers."

> Saviour, I know thy gracious will,
> Thou waitest for admittance still,
> Thy knock, thy mercy's voice I hear,
> And open wide my heart sincere,
> I use the power my Lord doth give,
> And gladly now thyself receive.
>
> Enter with all thy fulness in,
> And cast out this intruder sin,
> Challenge thy dear-bought property,
> And pleas'd with what thou bring'st to me,
> (The good which comes from thee alone)
> Vouchsafe to banquet on thine own.
>
> Nothing have I to offer thee
> But wretchedness and poverty:
> O would'st thou in thy servant find
> The lowly, meek, and patient mind,
> Dispread thine image o'er my breast,
> And on thy own perfection feast.
>
> Then should I with my Saviour sup,
> To the third heaven at last caught up,
> Obtain the bliss begun below,
> (The bliss I now would die to know)
> Sit down, O king of saints, with thee,
> And feast to all eternity.
>
> (*Scripture Hymns*, vol. 2, Hymn 847)

Reflect

How do we wait for the Lord? In the early years of the Wesleyan revival, this question surfaced with force. Some, convinced that there was nothing they could do to obtain salvation since it was God's gift, advocated doing nothing at all. "Be still," they argued. "Do nothing, or you will rely on what you do for your salvation." This translated concretely into the commands, "Do not pray. Do not read scripture. Do not worship"—literally, just wait for God to do something to you. This disturbed the Wesleys tremendously. Against these advocates of "stillness," they admonished their followers to immerse themselves in the means of grace. Wait, in other words, in those practices where God has promised to meet us. Pray. Read the word of God. Join in fellowship. Receive Eucharist. Over against a passive approach to waiting on God, they advocated an active spirituality. If you want to meet God, open the door behind which God stands.

The Scripture and the hymn both use this imagery to communicate the same message and extend it even further. Both link the image of opening a door to the vision of a meal. These symbols reflect the importance of intimacy in our lives. As Wesley plays with the metaphors, he turns the concept of waiting on its head. We wait in the season of Advent, but there is also a sense in which the Lord waits on us. God calls us to action. Wesley clarifies that even the ability to act—to open the door—comes from God. God never coerces; God graciously provides. Grace responds to grace as God translates our faith into action. Once permitted entry, the Spirit lovingly works on our souls. Darkness and evil need to be expelled so that love can take up residence in every corner and fill our lives. God lays a banquet before us and it is a feast of perfect love. Hope springs to life as we contemplate the eternal feast—the heavenly banquet anticipated in every eucharistic meal.

At a conference at Keble College, Oxford, I took advantage of the opportunity to meditate every morning before William Holman Hunt's famous painting *The Light of the World*. In this masterpiece, Christ stands, knocking on a door representative of the human heart. In addition to the masterful depiction of light, the most memorable feature of the painting is the absence of any outside knob or latch on the door. The door must be opened from within. Christ will not force his way inside.

Pray

Patient Lord, through your grace, enable me to open my life to you so that you might come in and dwell with me and that I might feast with you forever. Amen.

SATURDAY IN ADVENT I

Read

> For whatever was written in former days was written for our instruction, so that by steadfastness and by the encouragement of the scriptures we might have hope. May the God of steadfastness and encouragement grant you to live in harmony with one another, in accordance with Christ Jesus, so that together you may with one voice glorify the God and Father of our Lord Jesus Christ. (Romans 15:4–6)

Sing

Unusual Meter: 555 11

> Away with our fears:
> The Godhead appears,
> In Christ reconciled,
> The Father of Mercies in Jesus the child.

> He comes from above,
> In manifest love,
> The desire of our eyes,
> The meek Lamb of God in a manger he lies.

> At Immanuel's birth
> What a triumph on earth,
> Yet could it afford
> No better a place for its heavenly Lord!

> The Ancient of Days,
> To redeem a lost race,
> From his glory comes down,
> Self-humbled to carry us up to a crown.

> Made flesh for our sake,
> That we might partake,
> The nature divine,
> And again in his image, his holiness shine;

As heavenly birth,
Experience on earth,
And rise to his throne,
And live with our Jesus eternally one.

Then let us believe,
And gladly receive
The tidings they bring,
Who publish to sinners, their Saviour and King.

And while we are here,
Our King shall appear,
His Spirit impart,
And form his full image of love in our heart.

(*Nativity Hymns*, Hymn 8)

Reflect

How do you handle discouragement? Do you ever feel alone, forgotten, invisible? Have you ever felt the burden of standing up for what is right and true and pure? Oppressed, ostracized, distressed, does spiritual exhaustion ever overtake you? Waiting, and looking, and waiting some more, do you ever question, What was I waiting for in the first place? Do you ever wonder if it is worth it? Is there any hope?

Some within the Christian community of Rome must have experienced these feelings. Otherwise, St. Paul would not have felt compelled to write as he does toward the end of his letter to this expanding group of people trying to live in Christ. In chapter 14 he reminds his friends not to judge one another. "Don't trip people up," he admonishes, "for we are to clear a path for others, not put obstacles in their way." He turns his attention to building up the neighbor, and his train of thought leads him seamlessly into prayer: "May the God of steadfastness and encouragement grant you to live in harmony with one another, in accordance with Christ Jesus, so that together you may with one voice glorify the God and Father of our Lord Jesus Christ."

God encourages people in their waiting and in their working. God remains steadfast, despite the way others may ignore or abandon us. When God comes—when we respond to God's embrace—we sing.

Though we are many, we sing as one, because it is a song to the glory of God that unites our hearts and voices. Life becomes a song to sing: a harmonized melody through which to praise God. Charles Wesley must have had something like this in mind as he contemplated the coming of Christ. He wrote "Away with our fears" in an unusual, galloping meter. Read through the hymn again and allow it to carry you away from fear and doubt through rhythm and sound. By coming to us in Christ, God demonstrates steadfast love, encourages, fulfills, triumphs, redeems, elevates. God restores hope and fills us with love.

Pray

God of steadfastness and encouragement, as we await the coming of Jesus, lift our spirits and restore our hope, through the power of your Spirit, for we put our trust in you. Amen.

ADVENT II: YEARNING FOR PEACE AND LIGHT

SECOND SUNDAY IN ADVENT

Read

For a child has been born for us, a son given to us; authority rests upon his shoulders; and he is named Wonderful Counselor, Mighty God, Everlasting Father, Prince of Peace. His authority shall grow continually, and there shall be endless peace for the throne of David and his kingdom. He will establish and uphold it with justice and with righteousness from this time onward and forevermore. The zeal of the LORD of hosts will do this. (Isaiah 9:6–7)

Sing

Meter: SMD

This hymn can be sung to Diademata, the tune used for "Crown Him with Many Crowns."

>   Father our hearts we lift,
>   Up to thy gracious throne,

And bless thee for the precious gift,
  Of thine incarnate Son:
The gift unspeakable,
  We thankfully receive,
And to the world thy goodness tell,
  And to thy glory live.

Jesus, the holy child,
  Doth by his birth declare,
That God and man are reconciled,
  And one in him we are:
Salvation through his name
  To all mankind is given,
And loud his infant cries proclaim,
  A peace 'twixt earth and heaven.

A peace on earth he brings,
  Which never more shall end:
The Lord of hosts, the King of Kings,
  Declares himself our friend;
Assumes our flesh and blood,
  That we his Spirit may gain;
That everlasting Son of God,
  The mortal Son of man.

His kingdom from above,
  He doth to us impart,
And pure benevolence and love,
  O'erflow the faithful heart:
Changed in a moment we
  The sweet attraction find,
With open arms of charity
  Embracing all mankind.

O might they all receive,
  The new-born Prince of peace
And meekly in his spirit live,

And in his love increase!
Till he convey us home,
Cry every soul aloud,
Come, thou desire of nations come,
And take us up to God.

(*Nativity Hymns*, Hymn 9)

Reflect

Human beings yearn for many things in life. In these days of terror, violence, genocide, and war, my suspicion is that most people desire peace more than anything else. Peace of heart. Peace of mind. Peace in families. Peace in our world. Peace. The prophet Isaiah describes the Messiah: Wonderful Counselor, Mighty God, Everlasting Father, Prince of Peace. This child born for us all brings no ordinary peace to us and to our world. He inaugurates an era of "endless peace," a peace built upon the foundations of justice and righteousness. He embodies shalom. We yearn for this shalom. We ache for it.

Wesley alludes to peace twice in the hymn for today, in addition to Jesus' title. Each reference draws us into the center of God's vision for our lives and God's world. He refers to a "peace 'twixt earth and heaven." Until restless hearts find rest in God, there is little hope of peace in any aspect of life. Wesley points first to a vertical dimension of peace—restored relationship with God. He describes Jesus as "the gift unspeakable" because the incarnation begins the process of healing our broken relationship with God. The birth of this holy child itself declares "that God and [God's children] are reconciled." Inner peace—reconciliation with God—precedes all other forms of peace for which we yearn.

But the Son of God also brings "peace on earth." Wounded hearts healed by God yearn to offer themselves for the peace of others. Those befriended by the King of Kings are captured by the vision of friendship that crosses all boundaries and reconciliation that brings global peace. God grants this peace as a gift. God imparts a desire to love, and this passion overflows faithful hearts, transforms people, and embraces everyone. Wesley prays that all people might receive this newborn Prince of Peace that peace might rule in the hearts of all people and reign on earth. This peace begins with you.

Pray

Prince of Peace, establish your rule of love in my heart and use me as an instrument of your peace in some way this day so that others might be drawn into your wide embrace. Amen.

Monday in Advent II

Read

Will you not revive us again, so that your people may rejoice in you? Show us your steadfast love, O Lord, and grant us your salvation. Let me hear what God the Lord will speak, for he will speak peace to his people, to his faithful, to those who turn to him in their hearts. Surely his salvation is at hand for those who fear him, that his glory may dwell in our land. Steadfast love and faithfulness will meet; righteousness and peace will kiss each other. (Psalm 85:6–10)

Sing

Meter: LM

This hymn can be sung to Cornish, the tune used for "Spirit of Mercy, Truth, and Love."

> All glory to God in the sky,
> > And peace upon earth be restored!
> O Jesus, exalted on high,
> > Appear, our omnipotent Lord!
> Who meanly in Bethlehem born,
> > Didst stoop to redeem a lost race,
> Once more to thy creatures return,
> > And reign in thy kingdom of grace.
>
> When thou in our flesh didst appear
> > All nature acknowledged thy birth:
> Arose the acceptable year,
> > And heaven was opened on earth;
> Receiving its Lord from above,
> > The world was united to bless,

The giver of concord and love,
    The Prince and the Author of peace.

O would'st thou again be made known,
    Again in thy Spirit descend,
And set up in each of thine own,
    A kingdom that never shall end?
Thou only art able to bless,
    And make the glad nation obey,
And bid the dire enmity cease,
    And bow the whole world to thy sway.

Come then to thy servants again,
    Who long thy appearing to know,
Thy quiet and peaceable reign
    In mercy establish below:
All sorrow before thee shall fly,
    And anger and hatred be o'er,
And envy and malice shall die,
    And discord afflict us no more.

No horrid alarum of war,
    Shall break our eternal repose,
No sound of the trumpet is there,
    Where Jesus's spirit o'er flows:
Appeas'd by the charms of thy grace,
    We all shall in amity join,
And kindly each other embrace,
    And love with a passion like thine.
                    (*Nativity Hymns*, Hymn 18)

Reflect

The Psalmist provides two powerful images related to peace. First, God "speaks" peace to the faithful. Second, the "kiss" of righteousness and peace characterizes the salvation that is at hand.

God speaks and all that exists came into being from nothing. A word proceeds from God's mouth and something marvelous happens. "In the beginning was the Word, and the Word was with God, and the

Word was God" (John 1:1). God's speech, unlike a lot of human speech, creates, constructs, builds. The Word—God come to us in the flesh—extends this creative activity by offering re-creation to all people.

We tend to talk about the "kiss of death." A word spoken at the wrong moment. A secret relationship discovered. A wrong move. "Kisses of death," we say. But God reveals a whole other world—a unique vision of peace with justice. In this renewed world, a life-giving kiss intimately connects righteousness with peace. This different kind of kiss restores life rather than acting as a harbinger of death.

Charles Wesley describes the new world of God's design as a kingdom of grace. Heaven opens on earth with the descent of the Prince, who is also the Author of Peace. "In the beginning was peace, and peace was with God, and this peace was God." The Christ is not only an ambassador of peace, he is Peace. God calls us to live into the peaceable vision revealed and manifest in the person of Jesus—a world in which all sorrow flies away, anger and hatred disappear, envy and malice die, discord no longer afflicts us in any way; no war cry, no call to battle stations; rather, all people embrace and love as God loves.

Pray

Author of Peace, come to your servants again who long to see you, to know you, and to love you; establish your peaceable reign, for your mercy's sake. Amen.

Tuesday in Advent II

Read

For he is our peace; in his flesh he has made both groups into one and has broken down the dividing wall, that is, the hostility between us. He has abolished the law with its commandments and ordinances, that he might create in himself one new humanity in place of the two, thus making peace, and might reconcile both groups to God in one body through the cross, thus putting to death that hostility through it. So he came and proclaimed peace to you who were far off and peace to those who were near. (Ephesians 2:14–17)

Sing

Meter: 76.76.77.76

This hymn can be sung to Amsterdam, the tune used for "Praise the Lord Who Reigns Above" in some hymnals.

> Glory be to God on high,
>   And peace on earth descend:
> God comes down; he bows the sky,
>   And shews himself our friend!
> God, the invisible, appears,
>   God, the blest, the great I AM,
> Sojourns in this vale of tears,
>   And Jesus is his name.
>
> Him the angels all adored,
>   Their Maker and their King;
> Tidings of their humbled Lord,
>   They now to mortals bring;
> Emptied of his majesty,
>   Of his dazzling glories shorn,
> Being's source begins to be,
>   And God himself is born!
>
> See the eternal Son of God,
>   A mortal son of man,
> Dwelling in an earthly clod,
>   Whom heaven cannot contain!
> Stand amazed, ye heavens, at this!
>   See the Lord of earth and skies!
> Humbled to the dust he is,
>   And in a manger lies!
>
> We the sons of men rejoice,
>   The Prince of peace proclaim,
> With heaven's host lift up our voice,
>   And shout Immanuel's name:
> Knees and hearts to him we bow,
>   Of our flesh and of our bone,

Jesus is our brother now,
And God is all our own!

(*Nativity Hymns*, Hymn 4)

Reflect

Not long ago I was in South Korea at a major international conference. On the Sunday of this event, a large group of us traveled to the Demilitarized Zone (DMZ) to pray for the reunification of the Korean peninsula. The service moved me deeply. The yearning of the Korean Christians for unity in their land, for healing and peace, impressed me beyond words. I will never forget the songs of reconciliation we sang, the prayers for restoration we prayed, and the tears shed for a people divided by ideology and politics and for families separated by barbed wire and concrete walls.

Our text for today figured prominently in that service, and I don't think these words of Ephesians 2 had ever sunk so deeply in my soul as they did that day: "In his flesh he has made both groups into one and has broken down the dividing wall, that is, the hostility between us." Through Christ, God creates a "new humanity in place of the two." God puts hostility to death by means of the cross. An African bishop claimed the promise of reconciliation in Christ for the Korean people. He invited us, not only to ponder God's gift of reunification, but to live it out in our lives, each day, through the power of the indwelling spirit of Christ.

Wesley opens his powerful hymn celebrating the peace that God offers us in Christ with a paraphrase of the *Gloria in Excelsis*, an exclamation he prayed with every eucharistic feast. But the One alone who is Holy, Lord, and Most High, is the One who humbled himself and took upon himself the form of a slave. True peace comes through this humility of Jesus. Echoing one of the earliest hymns of the church embedded in St. Paul's second chapter to the Philippians, Wesley describes the One who descends, comes down, sojourns among us. The great I AM, who has no beginning or ending, "begins to be" as a helpless infant. The One whom heaven cannot contain becomes a human being just like you and me. Read each of the stanzas of this hymn slowly, and pause to ponder each in turn.

The only force potent enough to break down the barriers of human hostility is the power of divine humility. The humbled Lord empties himself, comes, and in this power proclaims peace to those who are far off and to those who are near.

Pray

Humble Lord, you emptied yourself of all but love and lived among us that you might break down the walls of hostility that divide us, one from the other; grant us peace in our time and joy in your eternal reign. Amen.

WEDNESDAY IN ADVENT II

Read

Arise, shine; for your light has come, and the glory of the LORD has risen upon you. For darkness shall cover the earth, and thick darkness the peoples; but the LORD will arise upon you, and his glory will appear over you. Nations shall come to your light, and kings to the brightness of your dawn. . . . The sun shall no longer be your light by day, nor for brightness shall the moon give light to you by night; but the LORD will be your everlasting light, and your God will be your glory. (Isaiah 60:1–3, 19)

Sing

Meter: LM

This hymn can be sung to Old 100th, the tune used for "All People That on Earth Do Dwell."

> Arise, and shine with borrow'd rays,
> Bright in reflected lustre shine,
> Thy Light is come, the Sun of grace
> Appears in majesty divine,
> Jesus, that uncreated sun
> Is risen, in his church to stay,
> To make through thee his glory known,
> The glory of eternal day.
>
> While nations uninlighten'd lie,
> With darkness palpable o'erspread,

On thee the Day-spring from on high,
    The Lord his brightest beams shall shed,
Stampt with the sinless character,
    His praise thou shalt display below,
And putting on thy Saviour here,
    Jehovah's glorious image shew.

Drawn by thy grace the sons of night,
    The Gentile world shall come to thee,
And kings o'er-power'd with heavenly light
    Admire thy dazzling purity;
Soon as to thee their face they turn,
    They shall their royal state forget,
On earth look down with holy scorn,
    And lay their crowns at Jesu's feet.
                (*Scripture Hymns*, vol. 1,
            Hymns 1121, 1122, 1123)

Reflect

We all yearn for light. As if in a darkened room, we wait for our eyes to adjust, but strain for a glimmer of light from any direction. We anticipate the coming of the Light with this kind of focused attention in the season of Advent. Three separate stanzas drawn from Wesley's *Short Hymns on Select Passages of Scripture* (1762) paraphrase the Isaiah text about this coming light.

All of Wesley's poetry emphasizes the importance of images that relate directly to life. In these three lyrical expositions of the text, he emphasizes how the light relates to us and how we reflect the light in our lives. Illumination anticipates action. First, Wesley calls the singer to "arise and shine." But we do not generate light from anything we are or do. In fact, we can neither arise nor shine apart from God's previous action on our behalf. Rather, we shine with the luster of "borrowed rays." Because the Light has come, we are able to glow with a glory that is not our own. We reflect back to God what God offers to us as a gift. Notice Wesley's interesting use of "sun" imagery and the way it enhances these relational qualities. Jesus, the uncreated sun, rises, and through his rising, manifests God's eternal glory, through us. Amazing!

In the next two stanzas, Wesley extends these themes. The Lord sheds his brightest light on those within the community of faith, and having put on Christ, we become transparent to the glory of God that rules our hearts and lives. We delude ourselves if we imagine that God intends this light only for us! As Simeon sang (Luke 2:29–32), and as Wesley prayed most every day at Evening Prayer, this is "light for revelation to the Gentiles." We reflect Christ's light, not to show off, but to draw others—the entire world—to the glorious God of light and love.

Pray

Glorious Light, send us out in peace to reflect your radiance, for we have seen the salvation that you have prepared for all people and made available in Christ Jesus. Amen.

THURSDAY IN ADVENT II

Read

Jesus said to them, "The light is with you for a little longer. Walk while you have the light, so that the darkness may not overtake you. If you walk in the darkness, you do not know where you are going. While you have the light, believe in the light, so that you may become children of light." (John 12:35–36)

Sing

Unusual Meter: 886.886

> True Light of the whole world, appear,
> Answer in us thy character,
>   Thou uncreated Sun;
> Jesus, thy beams on all are shed,
> That all may by thy beams be led
>   To that eternal throne.
>
> Lighten'd by thy interiour ray
> Thee every child of Adam may
>   His unknown God adore,

And following close thy secret grace
Emerge into that glorious place
    Where darkness is no more.

The universal Light thou art,
And turn'd to thee the darkest heart
    A glimmering spark may find;
Let man reject it or embrace,
Thou offerest once thy saving grace
    To me, and all mankind.

Light of my soul, I follow thee,
In humble faith on earth to see
    Thy perfect day of love,
And then with all thy saints in light
To gain the beatific sight
    Which makes their heaven above.
                    (*Scripture Hymns*, vol. 2, Hymn 400)

Reflect

In the Wesleyan tradition, light often symbolizes God's grace. Charles Wesley believed that God extends grace to us before we are even aware of God's presence in—or claim on—our lives. He called this grace that comes before everything else "prevenient" or "preventing grace." In other words, God envelopes every person born into this world with grace. God surrounds us with expressions of love, care, support, and direction. Our problem rests not in God's absence; rather, it relates to our failure to recognize God's presence, mercy, and grace that are already in our lives. One of the functions of light, therefore, is to illuminate the actions and care of this gracious God so that we can clearly see and experience God's love.

Grace is relational. Essentially, the word *grace* connotes God's unconditional offer of relationship, a relationship based on God's prior love for everyone and everything in creation. Both the Scripture text, and the hymn based on it, underscore this gracious, relational dimension of God as light. When Jesus says, "The light is with you for a little longer," he refers to himself. He confirms the importance of his relationship to the disciples, not only for them, but to himself. He affirms the other. Jesus then gives two commands: walk in the light and believe in the light. These are not so much laws to be obeyed as they are a relationship to cherish. He says, in essence, "My sojourn with you is coming to an end, but continue to walk with me; do not abandon the journey into the light you have begun. You have entrusted your life to me; if you continue to trust, you will surely become God's children."

The most powerful aspect of this gracious calling, in my view, is the fact that God excludes no one. The light shines on all. God extends the invitation to every person. In Christ, all people have the power to become children of the light.

Pray

True Light of the world, shed your beams on every person, that, walking together and believing in you, all may be led to that glorious place where darkness is no more. Amen.

FRIDAY IN ADVENT II

Read

[Give] thanks to the Father, who has enabled you to share in the inheritance of the saints in the light. He has rescued us from the power of darkness and transferred us into the kingdom of his beloved Son. . . . [T]hrough him God was pleased to reconcile to himself all things, whether on earth or in heaven, by making peace through the blood of his cross. (Colossians 1:12–13, 20)

Sing

Meter: 87.87 D

This hymn can be sung to Hymn to Joy, the tune used for "Joyful, Joyful, We Adore Thee."

> Light of those whose dreary dwelling
> Borders on the shades of death,

Come, and by thy love's revealing,
    Dissipate the clouds beneath:
The new heaven and earth's Creator,
    In our deepest darkness rise,
Scattering all the night of nature,
    Pouring eye-sight on our eyes.

Still we wait for thy appearing,
    Life and joy thy beams impart,
Chasing all our fears, and cheering
    Every poor benighted heart;
Come, and manifest the favour
    God hath for our ransomed race;
Come, thou universal Saviour,
    Come, and bring the gospel-grace.

Save us in thy great compassion,
    O thou mild, pacific Prince,
Give the knowledge of salvation,
    Give the pardon of our sins;
By thy all-restoring merit,
    Every burthened soul release,
Every weary wandring spirit,
    Guide into thy perfect peace.
                (*Nativity Hymns*, Hymn 11)

Reflect

Darkness depresses and burdens people. "Light of those whose dreary dwelling" enunciates this theme almost all too well. One of the most difficult aspects of the Advent season is dwelling in darkness, waiting for the dawn of a new day, awaiting the inbreaking light. Charles experienced dark times in his life. The death of his son, an exceptional musical prodigy, brought his world to near collapse. He knew the pain of darkness. His experience of God's "absence" shaped his life as much as the celebration of God's glorious presence. His poetry reflects reality. No sugar coating. No nostalgic waves of superficial joy.

The imagery is painful. Life sometimes "borders on the shades of death." Clouds hang over us, blocking the rays of the sun. The rising sun must "scatter all the night of nature—our "deepest darkness." We require the light for our survival. The remainder of the hymn portrays light, not as an option or an addendum to life but rather, the singer pleads with God passionately for the gift of light—for salvation in all its fullness. "Every burthened soul" and "every weary wandring spirit" finds his or her salvation only in this source. Light imparts life and joy, chases away all fears, and cheers the heart. "Come," the singer pleads four times; save, give, release, and guide.

As St. Paul reminds us, God must rescue us from the darkness. Jesus plays no games with life. God plans and executes a mission to redeem the hostages of darkness and safely relocate them in the dominion of the Prince of Peace to share in the inheritance of the saints in the light.

Pray

Universal Savior, when darkness and sin overwhelm me, chase away my fears, forgive me, cheer my heart, and enable me to share in the inheritance of the saints in the light. Amen.

SATURDAY IN ADVENT II

Read

And even if our gospel is veiled, it is veiled to those who are perishing. In their case the god of this world has blinded the minds of the unbelievers, to keep them from seeing the light of the gospel of the glory of Christ, who is the image of God. For we do not proclaim ourselves; we proclaim Jesus Christ as Lord and ourselves as your slaves for Jesus' sake. For it is the God who said, "Let light shine out of darkness," who has shone in our hearts to give the light of the knowledge of the glory of God in the face of Jesus Christ. (2 Corinthians 4:3–6)

Sing
Meter: 66.66.88

This hymn can be sung to Lenox, the tune used for "Blow Ye the Trumpet Blow," repeating the final line of each stanza, as in some hymnals.

Let earth and heaven combine,
    Angels and men agree,
To praise in songs divine
    The incarnate Deity,
Our God contracted to a span,
Incomprehensibly made man.

He laid his glory by,
    He wrapped him in our clay,
Unmarked by human eye,
    The latent Godhead lay,
Infant of days he here became;
And bore the mild Immanuel's name.

See in that infant's face
    The depths of Deity,
And labour while ye gaze,
    To sound the mystery;
In vain: ye angels gaze no more,
But fall and silently adore.

Unsearchable the love,
    That hath the Saviour brought,
The grace is far above,
    Or man or angel's thought:
Suffice for us that God we know,
Our God is manifest below.

He deigns in flesh to appear,
    Widest extremes to join,
To bring our vileness near,
    And make us all divine;
And we the life of God shall know,
For God is manifest below.

> Made perfect first in love,
>   And sanctified by grace,
> We shall from earth remove,
>   And see his glorious face;
> His love shall then be fully showed,
> And man shall all be lost in God.
>
> (*Nativity Hymns*, Hymn 5)

Reflect

My theological mentor, Dr. Robert E. Cushman, told me on one occasion that his favorite text in the New Testament was 2 Corinthians 4:6. This confession of St. Paul demonstrates the intimate connection between creation and redemption. God does not do something different in sending the Son to us as Redeemer and Lord. God has always radiated light throughout the universe—always extended God's very self to all in love. The love that spoke this universe into being is the same Word that came to dwell among us in the flesh in the person of Jesus of Nazareth, to heal and restore. In the beginning, God said, "Let light shine"; in the middle, the Radiance of God—Christ our Lord— shines in our heart; at the end, all shall be lost (as Charles sings) in the glory of this Light.

St. Paul packs each phrase in his confession of faith with meaning. "Light shines out of darkness," and, as the writer of John's Gospel reminds us, nothing will ever be able to put it out. The Light shines in our hearts. Light penetrates to the center of our being. It reveals "the knowledge of the glory of God." The incarnation enables us to know God, not simply to know things about God. A reporter purportedly asked the wife of Albert Einstein if she knew and understood his mathematical formulas. She responded tersely and with a twinkle in her eye, "Oh no; but I know Albert." But how can we really know God, see God? If you really want to know God, look into the face of Jesus Christ. Read his story. Study his teachings. Follow his way. Jesus shines the light of God's countenance upon us all.

The language of Wesley's hymn helps us to bow humbly in wonder before this great mystery of incarnation. In Jesus, God is "incomprehensibly made man."

"Unsearchable the love."

Pray

God of unsearchable love, shine in my heart this day that I might see the light of the knowledge of your glory in the face of Jesus Christ, my Lord and my Light. Amen.

Advent III: Singing for Joy

Third Sunday in Advent

Read

Praise the Lord! Praise, O servants of the Lord; praise the name of the Lord. Blessed be the name of the Lord from this time on and forevermore. From the rising of the sun to its setting the name of the Lord is to be praised. The Lord is high above all nations, and his glory above the heavens. Who is like the Lord our God, who is seated on high, who looks far down on the heavens and the earth? He raises the poor from the dust, and lifts the needy from the ash heap, to make them sit with princes, with the princes of his people. He gives the barren woman a home, making her the joyous mother of children. Praise the Lord! (Psalm 113)

Sing

Meter: 10 10.11 11

This hymn can be sung to Lyons, the tune used for "How Wondrous and Great."

> Ye heavenly choir
>> Assist me to sing,
> And strike the soft lyre,
>> And honour our king:
> His mighty salvation
>> Demands all our praise,
> Our best adoration,
>> And loftiest lays.

> All glory to God,
>   Who rulest on high,
> And now hath bestowed,
>   And sent from the sky,
> Christ Jesus the Saviour,
>   Poor mortals to bless:
> The pledge of his favour,
>   The seal of his peace.
>
> (*Nativity Hymns*, Hymn 2)

Reflect

The title "sweet singer" befits Charles Wesley. Music and sacred song dominated his life. His nine thousand hymns and sacred poems reflect the lyrical atmosphere of his life and home. He was always watching, listening, reading, writing—attending to God's presence in Word, in creation, and events in life—to find the right metaphor, the proper image, the perfect word to plumb the depths of love divine. Life equaled poetry for Charles. It was not unusual for him to burst into the house, having leapt off his horse's back, demanding pen and paper so as not to lose a line, a verse, a full hymn he had composed on his return from preaching. You could almost say that for him Christianity was as much a song to be sung as it was a life to be lived.

As we move into this third week of Advent our mood shifts, and we begin to sense the exhilaration of a life-changing event. Joy begins to reverberate in our hearts and minds as the keynote of our life's song. It erupts in praise, not unlike the psalmist who bursts with joy at the remembrance of the Lord. The praise of the Lord never ceases. God's children fill the entire day with praise, from the rising to the setting of the sun. Morning and Evening Prayer for Wesley established the parameters of a day filled with praise and wonder at the glory of God.

Most notably, faithful disciples praise the Lord because God "raises the poor from the dust, and lifts the needy from the ash heap." This God cares. In Christ we see the compassion of this One who notices the most vulnerable, the poorest of the poor. The Lord "gives the barren woman a home, making her the joyous mother of children." The Lord is blessed indeed! Praise the Lord! So Charles calls upon the assistance of the "heavenly choir," because our songs of praise are just not adequate as a response to the glory of this God. God's mighty acts of love elicit our best adoration—the entirety of our lives and a community of praise.

Pray

Blessed God, we praise your name from morning to night, because we see how your love extends to every living thing. May our lives be never ending songs of praise to you. Amen.

Monday in Advent III

Read

In the sixth month the angel Gabriel was sent by God to a town in Galilee called Nazareth, to a virgin engaged to a man whose name was Joseph, of the house of David. The virgin's name was Mary. And he came to her and said, "Greetings, favored one! The Lord is with you." But she was much perplexed by his words and pondered what sort of greeting this might be. The angel said to her, "Do not be afraid, Mary, for you have found favor with God. And now, you will conceive in your womb and bear a son, and you will name him Jesus. He will be great, and will be called the Son of the Most High, and the Lord God will give to him the throne of his ancestor David. He will reign over the house of Jacob forever, and of his kingdom there will be no end." (Luke 1:26–33)

Sing

Meter: 66.66.888

This hymn can be sung to Rhosymedre, the tune used for "Our Father, by Whose Name," repeating the final line of each stanza.

The solemn hour is come
For God made visible,
Fruit of a virgin's womb
A man with men to dwell,

The Saviour of the world t'appear
And found his heavenly kingdom here.

The sinners' Sacrifice,
   The Head of angels see
From Jesse's stem arise,
   And grasp the Deity!
His sacred flesh the only shrine
That holds Immensity Divine.

Let all mankind abase
   Their souls before the Lord,
And humbly prostrate, praise
   The great incarnate Word,
And welcome Jesus from above
With joy, and gratitude, and love.
                    (*Unpublished Hymns*, vol. 2, pp. 75–76)

Reflect

The angel Gabriel visits Mary in Nazareth and announces the birth of Jesus. Time stands still. It fills up as the significance of this proclamation sinks in. Gabriel confronts Mary with an inexplicable mystery and a daunting opportunity; the cosmos hangs in suspense, awaiting her response. If you are ever in Antwerp, Belgium, visit St. Paul's Church there and proceed to the north side aisle. You will discover fifteen paintings depicting the so-called mysteries of the life of Jesus, all inspired, in one way or another, by Rubens. The very first masterpiece, and the first of the "joyous mysteries," is Hendrik van Balen's rendition of The Annunciation. We stand face to face with the most amazing first in human history. Existing before time began, Jesus, the second person of the Trinity, begins to exist at a moment in time. The Lord of the universe begins to take on the nature of a servant. As Charles Wesley sings: "His sacred flesh the only shrine That holds Immensity Divine."

He opens his hymn with the simple but profound words, "The solemn hour is come." God takes the initial step to become fully visible, profoundly tangible, to enter human history as a human infant.

Having determined to come before the foundations of the world, God now acts to make that advent happen. God comes to comfort the wounded, to ransom the captive. In this incarnate One, God offers freedom for the condemned and salvation for all the sons and daughters of Adam and Eve, the entire human family. All creation groaned for this moment and now awaits the Virgin's response: "Here am I, the servant of the Lord," the humble handmaid replies, "let it be with me according to your word." The song of life begins!

Pray

Immensity Divine, fill us with humility, gratitude, and great love because of what you accomplished in the incarnation, so that we might live as your servants in the world. Amen.

TUESDAY IN ADVENT III

Read

And Mary said, "My soul magnifies the Lord, and my spirit rejoices in God my Savior, for he has looked with favor on the lowliness of his servant. Surely, from now on all generations will call me blessed; for the Mighty One has done great things for me, and holy is his name. His mercy is for those who fear him from generation to generation. He has shown strength with his arm; he has scattered the proud in the thoughts of their hearts. He has brought down the powerful from their thrones, and lifted up the lowly; he has filled the hungry with good things, and sent the rich away empty. He has helped his servant Israel, in remembrance of his mercy, according to the promise he made to our ancestors, to Abraham and to his descendants forever." (Luke 1:46–55)

Sing

Unusual Meter: 886.886

> The God of faithfulness and love,
> His mercy and his truth to prove,

> Hath call'd his word to mind,
> Hath succour on the Mighty laid,
> And sent in Christ his saving aid
> To us, and all mankind.
>
> He hath his promises fulfil'd,
> Jesus is in our flesh reveal'd
> To every sinner given,
> And all of Abraham's lot possest
> May live emphatically blest
> With pardon, grace, and heaven.
> (*Unpublished Hymns*, vol. 2, p. 77)

Reflect

St. Luke fills the early pages of his gospel with hymns. The "Magnificat," Mary's Song, stands out among them all as an eloquent statement of humility and obedience. Composers from Bach to Vivaldi have attempted to capture the essence of her lyrical confession of faith for the ages. It possesses a timeless beauty. Hardly sentimental, this prayer expresses the most central tenets of the way of Jesus.

Charles Wesley emphasized the autobiographical nature of faith. A "true and lively faith," to use the language of his Anglican heritage, will always express itself as "my faith." Faith is personal, intimate; not simply an object or set of propositions to which one subscribes. Mary's song begins in the first person singular. The mother of Jesus magnifies God in the most intimate terms: "*my* soul, *my* spirit, *my* Savior, will call *me* blessed, has done great things for *me*." Faith is personal trust. Mary celebrates the divine grace that has entered her life and captured her heart.

Although deeply personal, Mary's testimony is anything but solitary or individualistic. Her solo almost takes on the tone of a choir as she remembers and celebrates God's mighty acts of salvation, which culminate in the incarnation of the word of God. Seven verbs remind the community of the faithful about God's actions in human history: God has shown strength, scattered the proud, brought down the powerful, lifted up the lowly, filled the hungry, sent the rich away empty, and helped God's servant. These works of God demonstrate in concrete fashion how intimate God's connection is with the powerless, the humble, the lowly, the hungry, the poor, the servants, and the faithful ones who are pure and simple of heart. Wesley sings about this God of faithfulness and love—the God of promise who blesses with "pardon, grace, and heaven."

Pray

God of action, although Christ had but one mother, according to the flesh, form the Word anew in the souls of all your children, according to faith, that all people might believe. Amen.

Wednesday in Advent III

Read

O sing to the LORD a new song, for he has done marvelous things. His right hand and his holy arm have gotten him victory. The LORD has made known his victory; he has revealed his vindication in the sight of the nations. He has remembered his steadfast love and faithfulness to the house of Israel. All the ends of the earth have seen the victory of our God. . . . Let the sea roar, and all that fills it; the world and those who live in it. Let the floods clap their hands; let the hills sing together for joy at the presence of the LORD, for he is coming to judge the earth. He will judge the world with righteousness, and the peoples with equity. (Psalm 98:1–4, 7–9)

Sing
Unusual Meter: 8.33.6

> Angels speak, let men give ear,
>   Sent from high,
>   They are nigh,
> And forbid our fear.
>
> News they bring us of salvation,
>   Sounds of joy

To employ
Every tongue and nation.

Welcome tidings! to receive us
From our fall,
Born for all,
Christ is born to save us.

Born his creatures to restore,
Abject earth,
Sees his birth,
Whom the heavens adore.

Wrapped in swathes the immortal stranger,
Man with men,
We have seen,
Lying in a manger.

All to God's free-grace is owing;
We are his
Witnesses,
Poor, and nothing knowing.

Simple shepherds, us he raises,
Bids us sing,
Christ the King,
And shew forth his praises.

We have seen the King of glory,
We proclaim
Christ his name,
And record his story.

Sing we with the host of heaven,
Reconciled,
By a child,
Who to us is given.

> Glory be to God the giver,
> Peace and love
> From above
> Reign on earth forever.

(Nativity Hymns, Hymn 3)

Reflect

Before retiring each night, Charles Wesley would pull out The Book of Common Prayer and turn to "The Order for Evening Prayer." Following the general confession and absolution, the Lord's Prayer, the opening dialogue and the Gloria Patri, he read the appointed Psalter and Old Testament readings for the day. He then recited the portions of Psalm 98 that you read a few moments ago. Read the passage again. Wesley filled his heart and his life with these words every day. Can you just imagine how this ancient song shaped his life?

Sing to the Lord a new song. Celebrate the victory of God. Remember God's mercy and truth. Verse 4, in the Authorized Version from which Wesley read, proclaims: "Shew yourselves joyful unto the Lord, all ye lands: sing, rejoice, and give thanks." Sing. Rejoice. Give thanks. What an amazing testimony to the world this would be! And as in Mary's song from yesterday's readings, a mighty chorus joins us in our praise. Not a solo but a mighty chorus acts out God's praise. Not only the voices of men, women, and children fill the choir, but all creation joins in the song. We can imagine the "Angels and Archangels" and "all the company of heaven" magnifying God's glorious name in one great hymn of praise.

In anticipation of the coming One, the singers of the melody line exclaim, "Glory be to God the giver," and in harmony, the chorus of all God's people responds, "Peace and love From above Reign on earth forever." Unfortunately, Wesley's sacred poem is written in an unusual meter for which we have no tune. What a marvelous hymn it would be to sing! But read through it again as one who loves to sing, rejoice, and give thanks, and see what God does to your spirit.

Pray

Giving God, who never seems to tire of blessing the lives of your children: grant that we may sing a new song of thanks to you as ancient and enduring as your steadfast love. Amen.

THURSDAY IN ADVENT III

Read

I am the vine, you are the branches. Those who abide in me and I in them bear much fruit, because apart from me you can do nothing. Whoever does not abide in me is thrown away like a branch and withers; such branches are gathered, thrown into the fire, and burned. . . . As the Father has loved me, so I have loved you; abide in my love. If you keep my commandments, you will abide in my love, just as I have kept my Father's commandments and abide in his love. I have said these things to you so that my joy may be in you, and that your joy may be complete. (John 15:5–6, 9–11)

Sing

Meter: CM

This hymn can be sung to St. Agnes, the tune used for "Come, Holy Spirit, Heavenly Dove."

Jesu, united by thy grace,
   And each to each endeared,
With confidence we seek thy face,
   And know our prayer is heard.

Make us into one Spirit drink,
   Baptize into thy name,
And let us always kindly think,
   And sweetly speak the same.

Touched by the loadstone of thy love,
   Let all our hearts agree,
And ever towards each other move,
   And ever move towards thee.

To thee inseparably joined,
   Let all our spirits cleave;
O may we all the loving mind
   That was in thee receive!

Yet when the fullest joy is given,
The same delight we prove,
In earth, in paradise, in heaven
Our all in all is love.

(Hymns, Hymn 490.1, 3–5, 9)

Reflect

Even if the church agrees on the melody (which often is not the case), singing in tune and in perfect harmony presents unique challenges. Sometimes the church's song sounds more like a cacophony than a symphony. We seek to sing the song of joy, but our own interpretation of the theme, our own desire to shine, or our presumption get in the way. And yet, Christ calls for the faithful to sing together, to make music in one accord in praise of God. Jesus calls us into the practice of singing the song of life, together, as one.

The four stanzas of this more familiar hymn of Charles Wesley actually come from a much longer hymn of four parts, originally titled "A Prayer for Persons joined in Fellowship." The Wesleys elevated fellowship, or Christian conference as they called it, as an important means of grace. Along with prayer, study of Scripture, and Eucharist, they believed that this practice helped conform the faithful into the image of Christ. Jesus' image of the vine and the branches expresses this truth beautifully. Baptism grafts us into the one vine. We all drink in the same Spirit. The sacrament of belonging unites us with Christ and with each other. Wesley addresses this question of unity, particularly in this portion of his hymn on fellowship.

God's grace unites. Only as we seek to emulate the grace of God in our relationships can we hope to fulfill God's purpose. Built upon the foundation of grace, love then stabilizes and sustains community. Inseparably joined to Christ, our spirits cleave to one another. Conformity to the loving mind that was in Christ, and not agreement on every topic, govern life in the one vine. As Dorotheos of Gaza observed centuries ago, if we all seek a closer fellowship with Christ, then we will all move closer to each other as we move closer to him. If we abide in Christ and with one another in this way, then our joy will be complete and the harmonious symphony of our common life will bear witness to the One who unites us all.

Pray

True Vine, giver of life and sustainer of joy, draw us closer to you through the power of your Spirit, that we might embrace one another as brothers and sisters in one family. Amen.

FRIDAY IN ADVENT III

Read

Let the same mind be in you that was in Christ Jesus, who, though he was in the form of God, did not regard equality with God as something to be exploited, but emptied himself, taking the form of a slave, being born in human likeness. And being found in human form, he humbled himself and became obedient to the point of death—even death on a cross. Therefore God also highly exalted him and gave him the name that is above every name, so that at the name of Jesus every knee should bend, in heaven and on earth and under the earth, and every tongue should confess that Jesus Christ is Lord, to the glory of God the Father. (Philippians 2:5–11)

Sing

Unusual Meter: 886.886

> All-wise, all-good, almighty Lord,
> Jesus, by highest heaven adored,
>   Ere time its course began,
> How did thy glorious mercy stoop,
> To take thy fallen nature up,
>   When thou thyself wert man?
>
> The eternal God from heaven came down,
> The King of glory dropped his crown,
>   And veiled his majesty;
> Emptied of all but love he came,
> Jesus, I call thee by the name,
>   The pity bore for me.

O holy child, still let thy birth
Bring peace to us poor worms on earth,
    And praise to God on high!
Come, thou who didst my flesh assume,
Now to the abject sinner come,
    And in a manger lie.

Didst thou not in person join
The natures human and divine,
    That God and man might be
Henceforth inseparably one?
Haste then and make thy nature known
    Incarnated in me.

O Christ, my hope, make known to me
The great, the glorious mystery,
    The hidden life impart,
Come, thou desire of nations, come,
Formed in a spotless virgin's womb,
    A pure, believing heart.
                    (*Nativity Hymns*, Hymn 15.1–4, 7)

Reflect

In the second chapter of Philippians, St. Paul records one of the earliest hymns of the church. The text elevates the humility of Jesus and God's exaltation of the Son in consequence of his obedience and redemptive work. The second person of the Trinity accomplishes this great act of love on the basis of his "self-emptying." Some use the term *kenotic* to describe this hymn, based upon the Greek verb *ekenōsen*, which means "he emptied himself." This kenosis refers both to the self-emptying of Christ in the incarnation and to his obedience to the divine will that led him to death on the cross.

This vision of self-emptying shaped much of Charles Wesley's thinking about Jesus. The phrase "He emptied himself of all but love" figures prominently in many of his hymns. In the familiar hymn "And Can It Be," kenosis expresses the mystery of the incarnation:

He left His Father's throne above
(So free, so infinite his grace!),
Emptied himself of all but love,
And bled for Adam's helpless race.
(*Hymns*, Hymn 193.3)

Rather than attempting to explain the incarnation in philosophical terms, as if to master the inexplicable, kenosis describes the lengths to which God's love will go to reach us where we are. As Wesley writes in another hymn, "He emptied himself of all but love, And died to ransom *me*!" The ramifications of this divine self-emptying stagger the mind. God becomes one with us that we might become one with God. Christ empties himself of glory and eternity, of every divine attribute save one, the essence of God, which is love. Fully divine—all love and nothing but love—he enters our world of brokenness and sin, takes on our human nature, and makes it possible for God to incarnate love in us. "Emptied of all but love he came."

We yearn, therefore, for the mind of Christ. We seek to emulate the spirit of the One who emptied himself of all but love. We want love to be the essence of our lives. Through the Spirit, God plants and roots and fixes that mind in us: a mind that is quiet, gentle, and patient; noble, spotless, and loving; thankful, constant, and perfect. "Come, thou desire of nations, come."

Pray

Lord Jesus, you emptied yourself of all but love and became obedient, even to death on a cross, for me: just as you took on our human nature, root and fix your divine love in me. Amen.

SATURDAY IN ADVENT III
WISDOM FROM THE MOST HIGH (DECEMBER 17)

Read

But God chose what is foolish in the world to shame the wise; God chose what is weak in the world to shame the strong; God chose what is low and despised in the world, things that are not, to reduce to nothing things that are, so that no one might boast in the presence of God. He is the source of your life in Christ Jesus, who became for us wisdom from God, and righteousness and sanctification and redemption, in order that, as it is written, "Let the one who boasts, boast in the Lord." (1 Corinthians 1:27–31)

Sing
Meter: LM
This hymn can be sung to Rockingham, the tune used for "When I Survey the Wondrous Cross."

> Happy the man that finds the grace,
> The blessing of God's chosen race,
> The wisdom coming from above,
> The faith that sweetly works by love.
>
> Happy beyond description he
> Who knows, the Saviour died for me,
> The gift unspeakable obtains,
> And heavenly understanding gains.
>
> Wisdom divine! Who tells the price
> Of wisdom's costly merchandise?
> Wisdom to silver we prefer,
> And gold is dross compared to her.
>
> Happy the man who wisdom gains;
> Thrice happy who his guest retains;
> He owns, and shall for ever own,
> Wisdom, and Christ, and heaven are one.
>
> (*Hymns*, Hymn 14.1–3, 6)

Reflect
Today we begin our journey through the so-called "O Antiphons." In early monastic practice, the antiphons preceded the Magnificat in the Service of Vespers during the Octave before Christmas, from December 17 to December 23. While the exact origin of these prayers remains shrouded in mystery, liturgical use of the antiphons in Rome established their present form before the eighth century. Each invocation

highlights a title for the Messiah drawn from the prophecy of Isaiah. Of particular interest is the fact that, if the titles are reversed, the first letter of each spells out the Latin phrase *ero cras* (Emmanuel, Rex, Oriens, Clavis, Radix, Adonai, Sapientia), which means, "Tomorrow, I will come." The O Antiphons, therefore, not only intensify our Advent preparations but bring a special note of joy to our progress toward the eve of Jesus' birth.

The O Antiphons open with the messianic title "O Wisdom." In Isaiah's depiction of the peaceable kingdom ushered in by the Messiah, he proclaims that "the spirit of wisdom and of understanding" will rest on the coming One (Isaiah 11:2). More particularly, this is Wisdom that comes from the Most High. Human wisdom leads in one direction, divine Wisdom in another altogether. St. Augustine once claimed that God's wisdom turns everything upside down, and that is precisely what we find in the Scripture reading and the hymn for today. The world characterizes this wisdom as foolishness, weakness, lowliness; the world despises this wisdom. Charles Wesley, however, celebrates the wisdom that comes from above in one of his *Redemption Hymns*. Those who are captured by the Word know that "Wisdom, and Christ, and heaven are one." Indeed, Wisdom and the word of God are one. Just as Wisdom creates in the beginning, it is now "the source of your life in Christ Jesus." The Wisdom of the Most High brings righteousness, sanctification, and redemption to all who entrust their lives to her way.

Pray

O Wisdom, who came from the mouth of the Most High, reaching from end to end and ordering all things mightily and sweetly: Come, and teach us the way of prudence. Amen.

ADVENT IV: LIVING BY FAITH

FOURTH SUNDAY IN ADVENT
RULER OF THE HOUSE OF ISRAEL (DECEMBER 18)

Read

But you, O Bethlehem of Ephrathah, who are one of the little clans of Judah, from you shall come forth for me one who is to rule in Israel, whose origin is from of old, from ancient days. Therefore he shall give them up until the time when she who is in labor has brought forth; then the rest of his kindred shall return to the people of Israel. And he shall stand and feed his flock in the strength of the LORD, in the majesty of the name of the LORD his God. And they shall live secure, for now he shall be great to the ends of the earth; and he shall be the one of peace. (Micah 5:2–5)

Sing
Meter: LM
This hymn can be sung to Tallis' Canon, the tune used for "All Praise to Thee, my God, This Night."

> Ye simple men of heart sincere,
>> Shepherds, who watch your flocks by night,
> Start not to see an angel near,
>> Nor tremble at his glorious light.
>
> An herald from the heavenly king,
>> I come your every fear to chase;
> Good tidings of great joy I bring,
>> Great joy to all the fallen race.
>
> To you is born on this glad day,
>> A Saviour, by our host adored;
> Our God in Bethlehem survey,
>> Make haste to worship Christ the Lord.
>
> By this the Saviour of mankind,
>> The incarnate God shall be displayed,
> The Babe ye wrapped in swathes shall find,
>> And humbly in a manger laid.
>>> (*Nativity Hymns*, Hymn 1)

Reflect
When I first examined the text and the hymn appointed for this day, sentimental images of shepherds swirled in my mind, boys in bath-

robes on a makeshift hillside outside Bethlehem. The O Antiphon, however, snapped me back to reality and refused to cooperate with the trajectory of my thinking. Rather, it drew me, somewhat unwillingly, to the origin of this second messianic title: "O Lord and Ruler of the house of Israel." The full invocation conjures up frightening or awe-inspiring images: a burning bush, a holy mountain, a mighty hand outstretched to save. Moreover, one of the principal texts for the antiphon (Isaiah 33:21a, 22) proclaims: "But there the LORD in majesty will be for us. . . . For the LORD is our judge, the LORD is our ruler, the LORD is our king; he will save us." How does the image of a shepherd ruler—the Good Shepherd—square with these awful scenes and the overwhelming presence of God? Martin Luther purportedly observed that if in the presence of an earthly king we tremble, so how much more when in the presence of the Ruler of the universe.

I found the connections hard to make until I realized I needed a deliverer who was willing to face great danger to rescue me. I needed One who had the courage, wisdom, and power to secure my liberty and safety. It dawned on me that the shepherd's life was far from easy. The idyllic pastoral scenes can so easily blind us from the fact that shepherds faced danger daily. They laid their lives on the line to protect the flock—at least the Good Shepherd who truly cared for the sheep did. Wesley's hymn reminded me that angels proclaimed a gospel word to the shepherds so that they might "make haste to worship Christ the Lord." They paid homage to a King who possessed the divine power and authority to rule. He stands and feeds his flock in the strength of the Lord, in the majesty of the name of the Lord his God. We live by faith in him.

Pray

O Lord and Ruler of the house of Israel, who appeared to Moses in the flame of the burning bush and gave him the law on Sinai: Come, and redeem us with outstretched arm. Amen.

MONDAY IN ADVENT IV
ROOT OF JESSE (DECEMBER 19)

Read

A shoot shall come out from the stump of Jesse, and a branch shall grow out of his roots. The spirit of the LORD shall rest on him, the spirit of wisdom and understanding, the spirit of counsel and might, the spirit of knowledge and the fear of the LORD. His delight shall be in the fear of the LORD. He shall not judge by what his eyes see, or decide by what his ears hear; but with righteousness he shall judge the poor, and decide with equity for the meek of the earth. . . . On that day the root of Jesse shall stand as a signal to the peoples; the nations shall inquire of him, and his dwelling shall be glorious. (Isaiah 11:1–4, 10)

Sing

Unusual Meter: 76.76.88.76

> Branch of Jesse's stem, arise,
> And in our nature grow,
> Turn our earth to paradise,
> By flourishing below:
> Bless us with the Spirit of grace
> Immeasurably shed on thee,
> Pour on all the faithful race
> The streaming Deity.

> Let the Spirit of our Head
> On all the members rest,
> From thyself to us proceed,
> And dwell in every breast,
> Teach to judge and act aright,
> Inspire with wisdom from above,
> Holy faith, and heavenly might,
> And reverential love.

> Righteous judge, who read'st the heart,
> And know'st what is in man,

> Rise, to take thy people's part,
> The helpless cause maintain:
> Patron of the poor appear,
> Thy meek, afflicted subjects own,
> Manifest thy kingdom here,
> And call us to thy throne.
>
> (*Scripture Hymns*, vol. 1,
> Hymns 983, 984, 986)

Reflect

Do you know your lineage? Genealogy played an extremely important role in the ancient world. Roots established identity. Jesse was the father of King David, who was his youngest son. In Isaiah's time, when the tree of Israel had been cut down, when the people of God had been reduced to nothing more than a lifeless stump by exile and oppression, the prophet proclaimed that new life was coming. An advent of vitality approached. A shoot, he claimed, will come forth out of the stump, and a branch shall grow out of the roots. He called upon the people to put their trust in God, to live by faith, for restoration was just around the corner.

Wesley set this prophecy (Isaiah 11:1–4) to flight with an array of powerful images. God's restoration through the branch of Jesse's stem "turns our earth to paradise." Life not only returns but flourishes. It extends far beyond the bounds of Jesse and his line. The Spirit breathes life into the Son of David and rests upon all the faithful of his family, finding a home in every breast. The Messiah reads our hearts, knows us through and through, and rises to take up our helpless cause. He calls the poor and meek to his throne. He manifests the reign of God and invites us to live in it and for it in every way.

In baptism God grafts us into the root of Jesse. God reconstitutes us as living branches of the fruitful vine. The true vine nourishes and sustains us. We draw our life from him by faith.

Pray

O root of Jesse, who stands for an ensign of the people, before whom kings shall keep silence and unto whom the Gentiles shall make supplication: Come to deliver us, and tarry not. Amen.

Tuesday in Advent IV
Key of David (December 20)

Read

I will place on his shoulder the key of the house of David; he shall open, and no one shall shut; he shall shut, and no one shall open. I will fasten him like a peg in a secure place, and he will become a throne of honor to his ancestral house. And they will hang on him the whole weight of his ancestral house, the offspring and issue, every small vessel, from the cups to all the flagons. (Isaiah 22:22–24)

Sing

Meter: LM

This hymn can be sung to *Conditor alme siderum*, the tune used for "Creator of the Stars of Night."

> Where is the holy, heaven-born child?
>   Heir of the everlasting throne?
> Who heaven and earth hath reconciled,
>   And God and man rejoined in one?
>
> Shall we of earthly kings inquire?
>   To courts or palaces repair?
> The nation's hope, the world's desire,
>   Alas! we cannot find him there.
>
> Shall learning show the sinner's friend,
>   Or scribes a sight of Christ afford?
> Us to his natal place they send,
>   But never go to seek the Lord.
>
> We search the outward church in vain,
>   They cannot him we seek declare,
> They have not found the Son of man,
>   Or known the sacred name they bear.

Then let us turn no more aside,
    But use the light himself imparts,
His Spirit is our surest guide,
    His Spirit glimmering in our hearts.

Drawn by his grace we come from far,
    And fix on heaven our wishful eyes,
That ray divine, that orient star,
    Directs us where the infant lies.

See there; the new-born Saviour see,
    By faith discern the great I AM;
'Tis he! the eternal God; 'tis he
    That bears the mild Immanuel's name.

The Prince of Peace on earth is found,
    The child is born, the Son is given,
Tell it to all the nations round,
    Jehovah is come down from heaven.

Jehovah is come down to raise
    His dying creatures from their fall,
And all may now receive the grace
    Which brings eternal life to all.

Lord, we receive thy grace, and thee
    With joy unspeakable receive,
And rise thine open face to see,
    And one with God for ever live.
                                    (*Nativity Hymns*, Hymn 17)

Reflect

The image of the "key" figures prominently in two specific contexts of the scriptural witness; here, in the description of the Messiah as key of David (Isaiah 22), and in Jesus' words to Simon Peter concerning forgiveness of sins (Matthew 16). In both instances, as you might well expect, these keys have everything to do with opening and shutting, with binding and loosing. They relate ultimately to liberation, to the emancipation of captives from prison and of the faithful from the power of sin and death.

In ancient times, the chief royal steward would have a large master key of the palace fastened to the shoulder of his tunic. The key demonstrated his authority. No one would dare to question his action. Doors he closed remained closed; doors he opened remained opened. In the Revelation of St. John, the visionary writer applies this image to Christ Jesus, in whom, he believes, it is fulfilled: "These are the words of the holy one, the true one, who has the key of David, who opens and no one will shut, who shuts and no one opens: 'I know your works. Look, I have set before you an open door, which no one is able to shut'" (Revelation 3:8). An open door. A way forward. A secure entrance. The key opens a way for life.

Wesley's hymn opens with a flurry of questions that point, essentially, to one central query, Where can you find the key to life? You will not find answers, claims this lyrical theologian, in the corridors of power, in the great academies of the world, or even in the institutions that guard religious truth. Rather, rely upon the authority of the Spirit of Christ. The Spirit, "glimmering in our hearts," he claims, is our key and surest guide. The Spirit enables us "to discern the great I AM" by faith, in the face of "the new-born Saviour." The gloom of sin and sadness disburses and life displaces death when you put your trust in him.

Pray

O Key of David, and Scepter of the house of Israel, who opens and no one shuts, who shuts and no one opens: Come, and bring forth the captives from prison, those who sit in darkness and in the shadow of death. Amen.

Wednesday in Advent IV
Rising Dawn and Dayspring (December 21)

Read

"Blessed be the Lord God of Israel, for he has looked favorably on his people and redeemed them. He has raised up a mighty savior for us in the house of his servant David, as he spoke through the mouth of his holy prophets from of old, that we would be saved from our enemies and from the hand of all who hate us. Thus he has shown the mercy promised to our ancestors, and has remembered his holy covenant, the oath that he swore to our ancestor Abraham, to grant us that we, being rescued from the hands of our enemies, might serve him without fear, in holiness and righteousness before him all our days. And you, child, will be called the prophet of the Most High; for you will go before the Lord to prepare his ways, to give knowledge of salvation to his people by the forgiveness of their sins. By the tender mercy of our God, the dawn from on high will break upon us, to give light to those who sit in darkness and in the shadow of death, to guide our feet into the way of peace." (Luke 1:68–79)

Sing
Meter: 77.77.77

This hymn can be sung to Rastisbon, the traditional setting for this hymn.

> Christ, whose glory fills the skies,
> > Christ, the true, the only light,
> Sun of Righteousness, arise,
> > Triumph o'er the shades of night;
> Dayspring from on high, be near;
> > Daystar, in my heart appear.

> Dark and cheerless is the morn
> > Unaccompanied by thee;
> Joyless is the day's return,
> > Till thy mercy's beams I see;
> Till they inward light impart,
> > Cheer my eyes and warm my heart.

> Visit then this soul of mine;
> > Pierce the gloom of sin and grief;

Fill me, Radiancy divine,
Scatter all my unbelief;
More and more thyself display,
Shining to the perfect day.

(Hymns, Hymn 517)

Reflect

Zechariah and Elizabeth, kinsfolk of Mary and Joseph, presented their eight-day-old son for circumcision as was the custom. Ignoring all protocols at the naming, however, Elizabeth indicated that her boy was to be called John, not taking the name of his father; Zechariah concurred. Bewilderment seized the community and, immediately, John's father, who was mute, leapt to his feet and praised God in a prophetic song. The closing lines of his canticle inspire the themes of this day. "Through the tender mercy of our God; whereby the dayspring from on high hath visited us, To give light to them that sit in darkness and in the shadow of death, to guide our feet into the way of peace" (Luke 1:78–79 KJV). Morning dawns; the Dayspring appears.

Few sacred texts in the English language compare to the eloquent poetry of Charles Wesley's "Morning Hymn," more generally known by its first line, "Christ, whose glory fills the skies." Four ascriptions for Christ frame the opening stanza: Light, Sun of Righteousness, Dayspring, and Daystar. Jesus is the true *Light*, the only Light. The words of the Nicene Creed reverberate in our minds: "God from God, Light from Light, true God from true God." Looking with hope to the advent of the Messiah, Malachi prophesied that "the *sun of righteousness* shall rise, with healing in its wings" (4:2, emphasis added). In that day, God will tread down the wicked and heal the wounded. Nearly every day of his life, having taken The Book of Common Prayer in hand, Charles sang, "the *dayspring from on high* hath visited us," as part of Morning Prayer. The ascription *Daystar* derives from 2 Peter. The author admonishes the reader to heed "a light that shineth in a dark place, until the day dawn, and the day star arise in your hearts" (1:19 KJV). The subsequent stanzas of Wesley's hymn move the singer into deeper levels of intimacy with the One who cheers, warms, and visits us in the depth of our being, pierces our gloom, scatters our unbelief, and shines his divine light through our lives and into the world.

Pray

O Dawn of the East, brightness of the light eternal, and Sun of Righteousness: Come, and enlighten them that sit in darkness and in the shadow of death. Amen.

THURSDAY IN ADVENT IV
KING OF THE NATIONS (DECEMBER 22)

Read

So then you are no longer strangers and aliens, but you are citizens with the saints and also members of the household of God, built upon the foundation of the apostles and prophets, with Christ Jesus himself as the cornerstone. In him the whole structure is joined together and grows into a holy temple in the Lord; in whom you also are built together spiritually into a dwelling place for God. (Ephesians 2:19–22)

Sing

Unusual Meter: 77.44.7

> Join all ye joyful nations,
> Th'acclaming host of heaven,
> This happy morn,
> A child is born,
> To us a son is given.
>
> The messenger and token
> Of God's eternal favour,
> God hath sent down,
> To us his son,
> An universal Saviour!
>
> The wonderful Messias,
> The joy of every nation,
> Jesus his name,
> With God the same,
> The Lord of all creation.

The Counsellor of sinners,
Almighty to deliver,
  The Prince of Peace,
  Whose love's increase,
Shall reign in man forever.

Go see the King of glory,
Discern the heavenly stranger,
  So poor and mean,
  His court an inn,
His cradle is a manger.

Whom from his Father's bosom,
But now for us descended,
  Who built the skies,
  On earth he lies,
With only beasts attended.

Whom all the angels worship,
Lies hid in human nature;
  Incarnate see
  The Deity
The infinite Creator!

See the stupendous blessing,
Which God to us has given;
  A child of man,
  In length a span,
Who fills both earth and heaven.

Gaze on that helpless Object
Of endless adoration!
  Those infant hands,
  Shall burst our bands,
And work out our salvation;

Strangely the crooked serpent,
Destroy his works for ever,

And open set
The heavenly gate,
To every true believer.

Till then thou holy Jesus,
We humbly bow before thee,
Our treasures bring
To serve our King,
And joyfully adore thee:

To thee we gladly render
Whate'er thy grace hath given,
Till thou appear,
In glory here,
And take us up to heaven.

(*Nativity Hymns*, Hymn 6)

Reflect

The theme of "universal redemption" pervades the hymns of Charles Wesley. It functions like a cornerstone for his whole theology. We can locate the deepest roots of this central theme in the rich soil of the Hebrew people. God chose Israel. God called this tiny nation not to privilege but to responsibility. Whenever they forgot their mission, prophets reminded them of their proper vocation. God conferred upon this special people a responsibility to bear witness to the light. God called them to be a "light to the Gentiles." Through the chosen people, God manifested an inconceivable love for all. To the New Israel—the church—God confers the same gift, the same awesome responsibility. In Christ, God destroys all barriers that divide God's children; Jesus is King of the Nations.

Notice the universal call in the opening stanzas of Wesley's hymn. He invites "all the joyful nations" to join the heavenly host in acclaiming Jesus' birth. God sends a "universal Saviour." The Messiah is "the joy of every nation . . . the Lord of all creation." The Son of God excludes no one. He opens his arms to every people, race, and nation. Where else can anyone find such grace? We owe our homage to this King because we have encountered no such love in any other person or place. As the prophet Jeremiah observed centuries before: "There is none like you, O LORD; you are great. . . . O King of the nations. . . among all the wise ones of the nations and in all their kingdoms there is no one like you" (10:6, 7). Christ the King calls no one "stranger" or "alien"; in him, all are members of the household of God.

Pray

O King of the Nations and their desired One, the Cornerstone that makes both one: Come, and deliver your creatures, whom you formed out of the dust of the earth. Amen.

FRIDAY IN ADVENT IV
EMMANUEL (DECEMBER 23)

Read

[A]n angel of the Lord appeared to him in a dream and said, "Joseph, son of David, do not be afraid to take Mary as your wife, for the child conceived in her is from the Holy Spirit. She will bear a son, and you are to name him Jesus, for he will save his people from their sins." All this took place to fulfill what had been spoken by the Lord through the prophet: "Look, the virgin shall conceive and bear a son, and they shall name him Emmanuel," which means, "God is with us." (Matthew 1:20–23)

Sing

Unusual Meter: 66.77.77

Hail, everlasting Lord,
Divine, incarnate Word!
Thee let all my powers confess,
Thee my latest breath proclaim:
Help, ye angel choirs, to bless,
Shout the loved Immanuel's name!

Fruit of a virgin's womb,
The promised blessing's come:

Christ, the Father's hope of old,
  Christ, the woman's conqu'ring seed,
Christ, the Saviour, long foretold,
  Born to bruise the serpent's head.

He left his throne above,
  Emptied of all but love:
Whom the heavens cannot contain,
  God vouchsafed a worm to appear,
Lord of glory, Son of man,
  Poor, and vile, and abject here.

Hail, Galilean King!
  Thy humble state I sing:
Never shall my triumphs end!
  Hail, derided Majesty!
Jesus, hail! the sinner's friend,
  'Friend of publicans'—and me!
          (*Hymns*, Hymn 187.3–4, 7, 9)

Reflect

"God is with us." Emmanuel—the title of Christ in our final Advent Antiphon—is the most personal and intimate of all. In these past days our expectation has mounted, and now, this title confirms our deepest longings. God comes nearer to us than we could have ever imagined.

Emmanuel answers our deepest human needs: the need of daily salvation and forgiveness of our sins, the yearning to be at one with God, the desire for restoration and wholeness. Jesus overcomes all that stands between us and our Creator. "Christ, the Saviour, long foretold," sings Wesley, is "Born to bruise the serpent's head." No evil power can even stand in the way of love. As the angel explained to a bewildered Joseph, "You are to name him Jesus, for he will save his people from their sins." The title Emmanuel not only tells us about Jesus' mission, it reveals his nature. In Christ, God takes on our flesh. Mary gives birth to Jesus, a real person just like you and me; "For us and for our salvation he came down from heaven . . . and became truly human." But also, Jesus is "the only Son of God, eternally begotten of the Father . . . of one being with the Father." True God and true human dwell together in the One we call Emmanuel.

Nothing is left for us to do as we stand before this Savior, but to fall on our knees in awe and wonder as we confess, proclaim, and bless the "Divine, incarnate Word." "He left his throne above, Emptied of all but love," for *me*—for *all*!

Pray

O Emmanuel, God with us, our King and Lawgiver, the expected of the nations and their Savior: Come to save us, O Lord our God. Amen.

THE EVE OF THE NATIVITY OF OUR LORD
(DECEMBER 24)

Read

> In that region there were shepherds living in the fields, keeping watch over their flock by night. Then an angel of the Lord stood before them, and the glory of the Lord shone around them, and they were terrified. But the angel said to them, "Do not be afraid; for see—I am bringing you good news of great joy for all the people: to you is born this day in the city of David a Savior, who is the Messiah, the Lord. This will be a sign for you: you will find a child wrapped in bands of cloth and lying in a manger." And suddenly there was with the angel a multitude of the heavenly host, praising God and saying, "Glory to God in the highest heaven, and on earth peace among those whom he favors!" When the angels had left them and gone into heaven, the shepherds said to one another, "Let us go now to Bethlehem and see this thing that has taken place, which the Lord has made known to us." So they went with haste and found Mary and Joseph, and the child lying in the manger. (Luke 2:8–16)

Sing

Meter: 77.77 D with Refrain

This hymn can be sung to Mendelssohn, the traditional setting for this hymn.

Hark! the herald angels sing,
    "Glory to the newborn King;
Peace on earth, and mercy mild,
    God and sinners reconciled!"
Joyful, all ye nations rise,
    Join the triumph of the skies;
With th'angelic host proclaim,
    "Christ is born in Bethlehem!"

Christ, by highest heaven adored;
    Christ, the everlasting Lord;
Late in time behold him come,
    Offspring of the virgin's womb.
Veiled in flesh the Godhead see;
    Hail th'incarnate Deity,
Pleased with us in flesh to dwell,
    Jesus, our Emmanuel.

Hail the heaven-born Prince of Peace!
    Hail the Sun of Righteousness!
Light and life to all he brings,
    Risen with healing in his wings.
Mild he lays his glory by,
    Born that we no more may die,
Born to raise us from the earth,
    Born to give us second birth.

                (*HSP* [1739], pp. 206–8)

Reflect

"Why is this night different from all other nights?" That first Christmas Eve must have seemed ordinary for most people. There were meals to prepare, work to be done, children to get ready for bed, soldiers to avoid on the streets. Unrest and threats of violence were in the air, the consequence of injustice that crept into every corner of life. Conflict, terror, and oppression still ruled. It was an ordinary day.

In his musical drama about Charles Wesley entitled *Sweet Singer*, S T Kimbrough Jr. writes:

When nations rage with hatred and war, and innocent people are slaughtered for no cause; when humans terrorize one another in body and spirit and the clamor from the streets is but a massive cry of despair and groans of hunger; when there appears to be no reason for a child to be born to endure the insensibilities of life; when it seems that all is lost and there is no hope; there is still a song to be sung, a song which unites the music in every soul.[1]

> Hark! the herald angels sing,
>   "Glory to the newborn King;
> Peace on earth, and mercy mild,
>   God and sinners reconciled!"

More Christians sing this hymn at Christmas than any other carol. It circles the world like one great anthem of hope and joy. God's promise of peace radiates from the carol just as the exultant singing of the angels shone throughout the cosmos. The hosts of heaven glory in the birth of a new Deliverer, the merciful One, the Prince of Peace, who ushers in a reign of peace with justice for all. The reconciliation he offers provides the foundation of a new age. For those who suffer, who live in despair, who have lost all hope, he "rises with healing in his wings." Mary births this newborn King so that he might conquer, and raise, and give. But he comes not to conquer nations, rulers, or people; rather, he destroys the power of death. But he comes not to elevate himself; rather, "he lays his glory by" that he might lift us up as the children of God. But he comes not to condemn; rather, he regenerates us, breathes new life into us so that we might be whole. "Why is this night different from all other nights?" "Christ is born in Bethlehem!"

Pray

Come, Newborn King, come, and fix your humble home in my heart, that I might live in and for your reign of peace and love on the earth to the end of my days. Amen.

---

1. Copyright © 1985, rev. 1996, S T Kimbrough Jr. (privately published, nd), p. 45.

PART TWO

Hymns and Prayers for the Twelve Days of Christmas

WONDERING IN LOVE

THE NATIVITY OF OUR LORD

Read

In the beginning was the Word, and the Word was with God, and the Word was God. He was in the beginning with God. All things came into being through him, and without him not one thing came into being. What has come into being in him was life, and the life was the light of all people. The light shines in the darkness, and the darkness did not overcome it. . . . And the Word became flesh and lived among us, and we have seen his glory, the glory as of a father's only son, full of grace and truth. (John testified to him and cried out, "This was he of whom I said, 'He who comes after me ranks ahead of me because he was before me.'") From his fullness we have all received, grace upon grace. The law indeed was given through Moses; grace and truth came through Jesus Christ. No one has ever seen God. It is God the only Son, who is close to the Father's heart, who has made him known. (John 1:1–5, 14–18)

Sing
> Unusual Meter: 886.886

> What angel can the grace explain!
> The very God is very man,
> > By love paternal given!
> Begins the uncreated word,
> Born is the everlasting Lord,
> > Who made both earth and heaven!

> Behold him high above all height,
> Him, God of God, and Light of Light
> > In a mean earthy shrine;
> Jehovah's glory dwelt with men,
> The Person in our flesh is seen,
> > The character divine!

> Not with these eyes of flesh and blood;
> Yet lo, we still behold the God
> > Replete with truth and grace:
> The truth of holiness we see,
> The truth of full felicity
> > In our Redeemer's face.

> Transform'd by the ecstatic sight,
> Our souls o'erflow with pure delight,
> > And every moment own
> The Lord our whole perfection is,
> The Lord is our immortal bliss,
> > And Christ and heaven are one.
> (*Scripture Hymns*, vol. 2, Hymn 402)

Reflect

In a sacred poem based upon the prologue of John's Gospel, Charles Wesley explores the mystery of the incarnation. Today, we ponder the immensity of God's love and the incomprehensible act of God made human in the person of Jesus Christ. This gift truly inspires our awe.

The opening stanza of the poem explores what D. M. Baillie once described as the paradox of grace, something not even angels can explain. The God who created all that exists takes on flesh and enters human history. The uncreated Word, one with the Creator before time began, begins to be. He who is Alpha and Omega, the beginning and the end, from everlasting to everlasting, comes into this world, at a particular time, in a particular place, to a particular human family. The infinite, almighty God becomes a finite human creature.

The paradoxes continue. He is "high above all height," yet he dwells in the lowly form of a fleshly body just like yours and mine. The second person of the Trinity, who is Light and Truth—"immortal, invisible, God only wise"—becomes transparent in the son of a Galilean carpenter. We see the character of God in the face of this child. What shines through? We behold the truth of holiness and the truth of blessedness. We see a human life as God truly intends it to be lived. The vision transforms us. Once we have seen God in the face of Jesus we can never be the same again. This gift fills our souls as genuine blessedness overflows and takes possession of our hearts. We wonder in the love and know that this Jesus is our all in all: the goal of our living, the fullest happiness we seek, the reason we exist.

Pray

Word of God, made flesh in Jesus Christ, full of grace and truth: we can never comprehend the mystery of your incarnation, but we behold your glory and wonder in your love. Amen.

Feast of St. Stephen

Read

When they heard these things, they became enraged and ground their teeth at Stephen. But filled with the Holy Spirit, he gazed into heaven and saw the glory of God and Jesus standing at the right hand of God. "Look," he said, "I see the heavens opened and the Son of Man standing at the right hand of God!" But they covered their ears, and with a loud shout all rushed together against him. Then they dragged him out of the city and began to stone him; and the witnesses laid their coats at the feet of a young man named Saul. While they were stoning Stephen, he prayed, "Lord Jesus, receive my spirit." Then he knelt down and cried out in a loud voice, "Lord, do not hold this sin against them." When he had said this, he died. (Acts 7:54–60)

Sing
Meter: 88.88.88

This hymn can be sung to Surrey, the tune used for "Creator Spirit, by Whose Aid."

> Forth in Thy strength, O Lord, we go,
> Forth in Thy steps and loving mind,
> To pay the gospel-debt we owe,
> (The word of grace for all mankind,)
> To sow th' incorruptible seed,
> And find the lost, and wake the dead.
>
> 'Gainst these by Thee sent forth to fight,
> A suffering war we calmly wage,
> With patience meet their fierce despite,
> With love repay their furious rage,
> Reviled, we bless; defamed, intreat;
> And spurn'd, we kiss the spurner's feet.
>
> Arm'd with Thine all-sufficient grace,
> Thy meek unconquerable mind,
> Our foes we cordially embrace,
> (The filth and refuse of mankind,)
> We gladly all resign our breath,
> To save one precious soul from death.
>
> *(Preacher Hymns*, Hymn 2.1, 5–6)

Reflect
From the lofty language and images of John's Gospel and the glory of God in the face of Jesus Christ, we move to a rough, unwelcome scene of malice, hatred, and death on this second day of Christmas. The juxtaposition could not be more stark. We would much prefer to

bask in the overwhelming presence of angels and the transcendent splendor of God in human form, but life will not permit it. Rather, love will not permit it. Before we get lost in the sentimental, we do well to remind ourselves that the cross is already present in the cradle. The love that came to us on that glorious day later would be unrequited and nailed to a tree. On this day after Christmas day, therefore, the church demands that we examine just how far this love will extend through the remembrance of the first martyr of the Christian faith, St. Stephen. In his hymn, Charles Wesley describes the marching orders of God's grace-filled way of love.

The word *martyr* literally means witness. Martyrs, like Stephen, bear witness to their faith in Jesus Christ. In the meditation for Christmas day we celebrated the fact that our vision of God in Jesus transforms us. Once we have seen God in his face we can never be the same again. Stephen stands out as the first in Christian history to demonstrate the reality of this claim with his very life. Although tragic and heart-wrenching, the martyrdom of Stephen signals the triumph of God's love in a human life. Stephen's dying prayer rings throughout the ages, for here was a man fully transformed by the power of love. In his death we see that hatred does not win, evil cannot prevail, death will never have the final word. Tertullian, one of the great fathers of the early church, claimed that the blood of the martyrs is seed. The witness of Stephen must have planted an "incorruptible seed" in the heart of young Saul on that bloody afternoon, because it blossomed later in the life of St. Paul, a man conquered by a love that would not let him go. Just look what love can do!

Pray

Lord Jesus, transform my heart and soul through the indwelling of your love: Where there is darkness, let me sow light; where there is injury, pardon; where there is hatred, love. Amen.

FEAST OF ST. JOHN

Read

Love is patient; love is kind; love is not envious or boastful or arrogant or rude. It does not insist on its own way; it is not irritable or resentful; it does not rejoice in wrongdoing, but rejoices in the truth. It bears all things, believes all things, hopes all things, endures all things. . . . And now faith, hope, and love abide, these three; and the greatest of these is love. (1 Corinthians 13:4–7, 13)

Sing
Irregular Meter

> By faith we come
> To our permanent home
> By hope we the rapture improve;
> By love we still rise,
> And look up to the skies,
> For the heaven of heavens is love.
>
> What a rapturous song
> When the glorified throng
> In the spirit of harmony join!
> Join all the glad choirs,
> Hearts, voices, and lyres,
> And the burden is mercy divine.
>
> Hallelujah they cry
> To the king of the sky,
> To the great everlasting I AM,
> To the Lamb that was slain
> And liveth again—
> Hallelujah to God and the Lamb.
> (*Hymns*, Hymn 486.3, 5, 6)

Reflect
This third day of Christmas focuses our attention on the three great theological virtues of faith, hope, and love. St. Paul writes of these eloquently, of course, in his first letter to the Corinthians. These three words encapsulate the entirety of the Christian faith. God's mighty actions in the *past* reveal the unconditional *love* the Creator extends to all creatures. By *faith* we apprehend this love and embrace it in the

present moment. We live with *hope* in our hearts, anticipating the *future* consummation of all things in Christ.

"Christ has died." The act of creation, the deliverance of the people of Israel, and the incarnation all reveal God's love. We remember God's mighty acts, especially in the eucharistic Prayer of Great Thanksgiving, and God draws us through our remembrance more deeply into this love. But nothing reveals God's love more fully than the selfless act of God's Son on the cross. Love captures our hearts in the shadow of Jesus' cross.

"Christ is risen." We serve a living Savior. We entrust our lives to a present Master through the power of the Holy Spirit and become the companions of the One who will never abandon us. The gift of faith opens a new world to us as we relinquish our own desires and permit God to grasp us and transform us with a new vision of shalom. Faith liberates our hearts in the radiance of Jesus' presence.

"Christ will come again." According to St. Paul, love "hopes all things." Hope guides us into the future because of the love revealed in Jesus and the trust engendered by the indwelling spirit of Christ. We live toward the image of that great heavenly banquet in which all those who love God sit and feast at the table of love. Hope renews our hearts in the anticipation of Jesus' final victory.

Charles Wesley's hymn celebrates this wonderful vision of life in Christ, all present but not yet fully realized, in the manger of Bethlehem. Faith leads us home. Hope enraptures the spirit. Love elevates the soul. We sing a "rapturous song" with a "glorified throng," through a harmonious chorus that exclaims, "Hallelujah to God and the Lamb."

Pray

Lamb of God, who reveals the fullness of God through death and resurrection, bread and wine: gift me with faith, fill me with love, and inspire me with hope through all my days. Amen.

THE HOLY INNOCENTS

Read

Thus says the LORD: A voice is heard in Ramah, lamentation and bitter weeping. Rachel is weeping for her children; she refuses to be comforted for her children, because they are no more. Thus says the LORD: Keep your voice from weeping, and your eyes from tears; for there is a reward for your work, says the LORD: they shall come back from the land of the enemy; there is hope for your future, says the LORD: your children shall come back to their own country. (Jeremiah 31:15–17)

Sing

Meter: 77.77 D
This hymn can be sung to Aberystwyth, the tune used for "Jesus, Lover of My Soul."

> Father, by the tender name
>   Thou for man vouchsaf'st to bear,
> We thy needful succour claim,
>   We implore thy pitying care,
> For our stricken child distress'd:
>   Wilt Thou not our load remove,
> Calm the tumult in our breast,
>   Manifest Thy saving love?
>
> Human tears may freely flow
>   Authorised by tears Divine,
> Till Thine awful will we know,
>   Comprehend Thy whole design:
> Jesus wept! and so may we:
>   Jesus, suffering all Thy will,
> Felt the sort infirmity;
>   Feels His Creature's sorrow still.
>
> Life and death are in Thine hand:
>   In Thine hand our child we see
> Waiting Thy benign command,
>   Less beloved by us than Thee:
> Need we then his life request?
>   Jesus understands our fears,
> Reads a mother's panting breast,
>   Knows the meaning of her tears.

> Jesus blends them with His own,
>   Mindful of His suffering days:
> Father, hear Thy pleading Son,
>   Son of Man for us He prays:
> What for us He asks, bestow:
>   Ours He makes His own request:
> Send us life or death; we know,
>   Life, or death from Thee is best.
>   (*Family Hymns*, 73.1, 4, 6–7)

Reflect

The harsh realities of life intrude once again on this day of the Holy Innocents. The Gospel of St. Matthew records the unimaginable actions of King Herod following the birth of Jesus. He orders the death of all the children in and around Bethlehem who were two years old or younger. His insatiable thirst for power leads to acts of terrible cruelty. The event could not help but remind the faithful Jewish Christians of the lamentations of Rachel.

A baby is born. The Prince of Peace enters human history. At the same time, however, from all appearances, evil rules; innocent people suffer. Dark clouds begin to cast shadows upon this infusion of light and love into the world. Does this not reflect our life as well? The suffering of the innocents continues in our own time. Each day, as many as 30,000 children worldwide die from hunger and easily preventable diseases. Mothers refuse to be comforted because their grief is too great. What can we say in the face of such suffering?

Rather than try and explain this mystery, Charles Wesley prays to the One who entered our world of pain in Jesus Christ and stands with us in our suffering. He composed his hymn for a "Child in the Small Pox" in the midst of his own personal anguish. His own son, from all reports an amazing musical prodigy, lay at death's door. The pathos of his poetic prayer overwhelms us, but his trust in the one who "turns our mourning into joy" inspires us all the more.

God's own tears, he claims, authorize our grief. God feels the ache of the human heart through Jesus, who wept for those he loved and "Feels His Creature's sorrow still." The God we see in Jesus understands our fears and feels the anguish of our hearts. Jesus blends his tears with our own. Share the deepest anguish of your heart, this day, with the God who embraces us in our pain.

Pray

God of all who suffer, receive into the arms of your mercy all innocent victims; by your great might frustrate the designs of evil and establish your rule of justice, love, and peace. Amen.

Fifth Day of Christmas

Read

The law of the LORD is perfect, reviving the soul; the decrees of the LORD are sure, making wise the simple; the precepts of the LORD are right, rejoicing the heart; the commandment of the LORD is clear, enlightening the eyes; the fear of the LORD is pure, enduring forever; the ordinances of the LORD are true and righteous altogether. More to be desired are they than gold, even much fine gold; sweeter also than honey, and drippings of the honeycomb. (Psalm 19:7–10)

Sing

Unusual Meter: 55 11

O mercy divine;
O couldst thou incline,
My God, to become such an infant as mine?

What a wonder of grace,
The Ancient of days
Is found in the likeness of Adam's frail race!

He comes from on high,
Who fashioned the sky,
And meekly vouchsafes in a manger to lie.

Our God, ever blest,
With oxen doth rest,
Is nursed by his creature, and hangs at the breast.

So heavenly mild,
His innocence foiled,
No wonder the mother should worship the child.

The angels she knew
Had worshipped him too,
And still they confess adoration is due.

On Jesus's face
With eager amaze,
And pleasures ecstatic the cherubims gaze.

Their newly-born King
Transported they sing,
And heaven and earth with the triumph doth ring.

The shepherds behold
Him promised of old
By angels attended, by prophets foretold.

The wise men adore,
And bring him their store,
The rich are permitted to follow the poor.

To the inn they repair,
To see the young heir:
The inn is a palace; for Jesus is there.

Who now would be great
And not rather wait
On Jesus, their Lord, in his humble estate?

Like him would I be!
My Master I see
In a stable!—a stable shall satisfy me.

With him I reside;
The manger shall hide
Mine honour: the manger shall bury my pride.

And here will I lie,
Till raised up on high,
With him on the cross, I recover the sky.
(*Nativity Hymns*, Hymn 16)

Reflect

The ancient Hebrews founded their lives upon the Torah—meaning the "five books of Moses"—which are also the first five books of our Christian Scriptures. On this fifth day of Christmas we celebrate the Torah, the Law. Psalm 19 elevates God's Law and demonstrates its effects upon the faithful. The Law is perfect, sure, right, clear, pure, true, and righteous. It revives, educates, satisfies, enlightens, and endures. "Do not think that I have come to abolish the law or the prophets," Jesus once claimed. "I have come not to abolish but to fulfil" (Matthew 5:17).

A very close connection exists between the Law and Love. Yahweh actually gives the Law to the people as an expression of Love. The encapsulation of the Law in the Ten Commandments makes this clear. These laws demonstrate how to love both God and neighbor properly. If we desire the Law in the way the psalmist describes, that passion for what is right and good and true changes our lives. It aligns us with God's love and God's way.

Wesley's nativity hymn erupts with joy in a bounding but unusual meter. It rejoices in the mercy of God, the wonder of grace, the blessing of God. It rehearses the story of the birth, from the angels and the shepherds to the wise men at the inn. The power of the hymn, however, comes through the final stanzas and the turning point phrase, "Like him would *I* be!" Like the ancient Jewish Law, Jesus' new Law of Love transforms the heart. When we desire it more than anything else, we discover that God begins to dwell in our souls, that Christ lives in us, that the Spirit bears witness with our spirits that we are the children of God. We see the King of Glory in a stable, so "a stable shall satisfy *me*." In humility, the Savior sleeps in a manger, so "the manger shall bury *my* pride." Ultimately, like the One crucified because of his love for us all, so the cross shall shape *my* life. God writes the Law of Love on our hearts.

Pray

God of Sinai and Golgotha, who orients all things in the direction of Love: revive, educate, and satisfy my soul through your Law, that your Love might endure in my heart. Amen.

Sixth Day of Christmas

Read

O Lord, you are my God; I will exalt you, I will praise your name; for you have done wonderful things, plans formed of old, faithful and sure. . . . On this mountain the Lord of hosts will make for all peoples a feast of rich food, a feast of well-aged wines, of rich food filled with marrow, of well-aged wines strained clear. And he will destroy on this mountain the shroud that is cast over all peoples, the sheet that is spread over all nations; he will swallow up death forever. Then the Lord God will wipe away the tears from all faces, and the disgrace of his people he will take away from all the earth, for the Lord has spoken. It will be said on that day, Lo, this is our God; we have waited for him, so that he might save us. This is the Lord for whom we have waited; let us be glad and rejoice in his salvation. (Isaiah 25:1, 6–9)

Sing

Meter: 77.77

This hymn can be sung to *Nun komm, der Heiden Heiland*, the tune for "Savior of the Nations Come."

Sing, ye ransomed nations sing,
Praises to our new-born King,
Son of man our Maker is,
Lord of hosts and Prince of peace!

Lo! he lays his glory by,
Emptied of his majesty!
See the God who all things made,
Humbly in a manger laid.

Cast we off our needless fear,
Boldly to the church draw near,
Jesus is our flesh and bone,
God with us is all our own.

Let us then with angels gaze
On the new-born Monarch's face,
With the choir celestial joined,
Shout the Saviour of mankind.

Son of man, will he despise,
Man's well-meaning sacrifice?
No; with condescending grace
He accepts his creature's praise.

Will his majesty disdain
The poor shepherd's simple strain:
No; for Israel's Shepherd, he
Loves their artless melody.

He will not refuse the song
Of the stammering infant's tongue,
Babes he bears humanely mild,
Once himself a little child.

Let us then our Prince proclaim,
Humbly chant Immanuel's name,

Publish at his wondrous birth,
Praise in heaven, and peace on earth.

Triumph in our Saviour's love,
Till he takes us up above,
All his majesty displays,
Shows us all his glorious face.

(*Nativity Hymns*, Hymn 12)

Reflect

The traditional theme for this sixth day of Christmas is God, the Creator and Sustainer. Six refers to the days of creation. We celebrate, in the words of the psalmist, "plans formed of old, faithful and sure." The core idea for this day elevates our hearts and souls: God loves everything that God has created!

For those of us who try so hard and yet fail in so many ways, Wesley's hymn reminds us of this love, and even God's special choice of and mercy toward those challenged in one way or another in life. The Son of Man does not despise our inadequate, well-meaning sacrifice; rather, he accepts the simple praises of the people who join the ransomed nations in their song of gratitude to God. Israel's Shepherd does not disdain the crude nature of our gift; rather, he loves the simple and artless melody of our lives. The Savior of the world does not disregard our futile efforts to be eloquent in prayer or persuasive in argument; rather, he welcomes our faltering attempt to live as he lived, for peace, justice, and love on earth. Rather than ridicule us for our weakness or condemn the transparent brokenness of our lives, Jesus affirms the goodness of God's original creation in each of us and elicits our most noble qualities by displaying the majesty of his glorious face.

Moreover, according to the vision of Isaiah, God prepares a feast for us. Jesus invites us to be his table companions, and the vision of the banquet he prepares overwhelms us. He swallows up death forever. The Spirit wipes away the tears from all faces and removes all the barriers caused by our disgrace. "Let us be glad and rejoice in his salvation."

Pray

Creator God, who brought us to life and calls us good, even when we turn our backs on you: enable us to accept the fact that you have already accepted us for the sake of Christ. Amen.

Seventh Day of Christmas

Read

For as in one body we have many members, and not all the members have the same function, so we, who are many, are one body in Christ, and individually we are members one of another. We have gifts that differ according to the grace given to us: prophecy, in proportion to faith; ministry, in minister- ing; the teacher, in teaching; the exhorter, in exhortation; the giver, in generosity; the leader, in diligence; the compassionate, in cheerfulness. Let love be genuine; hate what is evil, hold fast to what is good; love one another with mutual affection; outdo one another in showing honor. (Romans 12:4–10)

Sing

Meter: 77.77

This hymn can be sung to Savannah, the tune for "Love's Redeeming Work is Done."

Christ, from whom all blessings flow
Perfecting the saints below,
Hear us, who thy nature share,
Who thy mystic body are.

Join us, in one spirit join,
Let us still receive of thine;
Still for more on thee we call,
Thee who fillest all in all!

Move, and actuate, and guide,
Divers gifts to each divide;

Placed according to thy will,
Let us all our work fulfil.

Many are we now, and one,
We who Jesus have put on;
There is neither bond nor free,
Male or female, Lord, in thee!

Love, like death, hath all destroyed,
Rendered our distinctions void!
Names, and sects, and parties fall,
Thou, O Christ, art all in all!

(Hymns, Hymn 504.1–2, 5, 9–10)

Reflect

Charles Wesley enjoyed equipping others for ministry. The movement he and his brother founded within the Church of England revolved around small groups called class and band meetings. In these intimate circles of accountable discipleship, men and women discovered their gifts and were encouraged to put them into practice in the mission of the church. The affirmation of the gifts bestowed on all by the Spirit fueled their revival of authentic Christian witness. These ardent Anglicans developed a reputation of "holding fast to what is good; and loving one another with mutual affection." Wesley rediscovered an organic vision of the church as the body of Christ in which all persons held special places of honor. His hymns elevated the unique giftedness of the people of God.

On this seventh day of Christmas we look at the seven gifts of the Holy Spirit as St. Paul describes them in 1 Corinthians 12. These include the ability to prophecy, minister, teach, exhort, give, lead, and offer compassionate service to others. Hardly restricted to the clergy, these gifts may be found among God's people in every parish in every age. Echoing Galatians 3:28, Wesley makes it clear in his hymn that there are no restrictions placed upon these gifts for those who have put on Christ. All distinctions dissolve in the community of faith. Wesley describes these gifts as blessings. When identified and practiced, these blessings lead the faithful into deeper levels of maturity, service, and love. The Spirit moves, actuates, and guides the use of these gifts in order that, together, we might realize God's mission in the world. The gifts perfect the saints. In this season of gifts, reflect upon how God has gifted you.

Pray

Blessed God, though we are many, we are one, because you unite us in Christ: open our eyes that we might discern and affirm the gifts you offer to us all through the Holy Spirit. Amen.

Feast of the Holy Name

Read

Blessed are the poor in spirit, for theirs is the kingdom of heaven. Blessed are those who mourn, for they will be comforted. Blessed are the meek, for they will inherit the earth. Blessed are those who hunger and thirst for righteousness, for they will be filled. Blessed are the merciful, for they will receive mercy. Blessed are the pure in heart, for they will see God. Blessed are the peacemakers, for they will be called children of God. Blessed are those who are persecuted for righteousness' sake, for theirs is the kingdom of heaven. Blessed are you when people revile you and persecute you and utter all kinds of evil against you falsely on my account. Rejoice and be glad, for your reward is great in heaven, for in the same way they persecuted the prophets who were before you. (Matthew 5:3–12)

Sing

Meter: 88.88.88

This hymn can be sung to *Vater unser im Himmelreich*, the tune for "Before Thy Throne, O God, We Kneel."

> Jesu, if still the same thou art,
>   If all thy promises are sure,
> Set up thy kingdom in my heart,
>   And make me rich, for I am poor:

To me be all thy treasures given,
The kingdom of an inward heaven.

Thou hast pronounced the mourners blest;
  And lo! for thee I ever mourn:
I cannot, no! I will not rest,
  Till thou, my only rest, return;
Till thou, the Prince of peace, appear,
And I receive the Comforter.

Where is the blessedness bestowed
  On all that hunger after thee?
I hunger now, I thirst for God;
  See the poor fainting sinner, see,
And satisfy with endless peace,
And fill me with thy righteousness.

Ah, Lord! if thou art in that sigh,
  Then hear thyself within me pray;
Hear in my heart thy Spirit's cry,
  Mark what my labouring soul would say;
Answer the deep unuttered groan,
And show that thou and I are one.

Shine on thy work, disperse the gloom,
  Light in thy light I then shall see,
Say to my soul, "Thy light is come,
  Glory divine is risen on thee,
Thy warfare's past, thy mourning's o'er;
Look up, for thou shalt weep no more."

Lord, I believe the promise sure,
  And trust thou wilt not long delay;
Hungry, and sorrowful, and poor,
  Upon thy word myself I stay;
Into thy hands my all resign,
And wait, till all thou art is mine!
       (*HSP* [1740], pp. 258–59)

Reflect

Today is the Feast of the Holy Name. We have already reviewed a number of names associated with Jesus in the O Antiphons during the concluding days of the Advent season. These only scratch the surface of the many titles and names for the incarnate One in the biblical witness. Some of the names of Jesus stand out immediately: Lord, Christ, Savior, Lamb of God, Shepherd, King, Word. Others remain more obscure and require study to unearth their roots, more often than not in the traditions of the Hebrew people: Lion of Judah, Man of Sorrows, Rose of Sharon. Jesus bears many names, none of them exhausting the wonder and mystery of his identity as the second person of the Trinity.

Of the many titles for Jesus, one of Charles Wesley's favorite epithets is the simple title, "Friend." This name of Jesus figures very prominently in his later hymns in particular, especially in the more expanded title, "Jesus, Friend of Sinners." More than anything else, Wesley experienced Jesus as his friend in life, his constant companion who stood by him in thick and in thin. When I was a young boy, my mother passed on to me what she described as her favorite book. It soon became one of mine as well and shaped my life in those formative years. In 1931 Leslie Weatherhead wrote *The Transforming Friendship* to reflect the way his friendship with Jesus had changed his life and deepened his faith in that which is divine.

Blessed are those whom Jesus befriends. In the Sermon on the Mount, Jesus described eight beatitudes. All relate in one way or another to the friendship that Jesus extends to all persons. Wesley's lyrical paraphrase of the Beatitudes—our hymn for today—expresses the yearning of the soul for true friendship with Jesus. This masterful text captures the human quest for intimacy with God. In one powerful couplet, Wesley expresses the desire of every heart: "Answer the deep unuttered groan, And show that thou and I are one." For Wesley, holiness is happiness; blessed is the one who is able to say, "Jesus is my Friend."

Pray

Jesus, whose name is above every name: open my heart and enable me to accept the gift of your transforming friendship and the blessedness of your presence, freely offered. Amen.

NINTH DAY OF CHRISTMAS

Read

By contrast, the fruit of the Spirit is love, joy, peace, patience, kindness, generosity, faithfulness, gentleness, and self-control. There is no law against such things. And those who belong to Christ Jesus have crucified the flesh with its passions and desires. If we live by the Spirit, let us also be guided by the Spirit. (Galatians 5:22–25)

Sing

Meter: 77.77 D

This hymn can be sung to St. George's Windsor, the tune for "Come, Ye Thankful People, Come."

> Come, thou high and lofty Lord,
> Lowly, meek, incarnate Word,
> Humbly stoop to earth again,
> Come, and visit abject man!
> Jesu, dear expected guest,
> Thou art bidden to the feast;
> For thyself our hearts prepare,
> Come, and sit, and banquet there.
>
> Jesu, we thy promise claim,
> We are met in thy great name;
> In the midst do thou appear,
> Manifest thy presence here!
> Sanctify us, Lord, and bless!
> Breathe thy Spirit, give thy peace;
> Thou thyself within us move,
> Make our feast a feast of love.
>
> Let the fruits of grace abound,
> Let in us thy mercies sound;
> Faith, and love, and joy increase,
> Temperance and gentleness;

Plant in us thy humble mind,
Patient, pitiful, and kind;
Meek and lowly let us be
Full of goodness, full of thee.

(*Hymns*, Hymn 506.1–3)

Reflect

In the fifth chapter of his letter to the Galatians, St. Paul enumerates nine fruits of the Holy Spirit: love, joy, peace, patience, kindness, generosity, faithfulness, gentleness, and self-control. These fruits constitute the portrait of a mature or authentic disciple of Jesus.

Charles Wesley connected these fruits of the Spirit with an early Methodist practice known as the Love-feast. The three verses of our hymn for today actually come from a much larger poem of twenty-two stanzas written specifically for use on these festive occasions. These feasts, rediscovered first in Wesley's day by Lutheran Pietists known as Moravians, reflect the Agapé tradition of the apostolic church. While the Eucharist celebrated the death and resurrection of Jesus, the Agapé, or Love-feast, developed into a less formalized fellowship meal centered in Christian witness and testimony. The original feasts were certainly full meals, but under the Wesleys' direction these events simply involved the use of water and bread. Sacramental in its feeling, but lay in its administration, a common loaf was often passed hand to hand and a "loving cup" with two handles developed for passing the water in similar fashion. Testimony was the heart and core of the Wesleyan Love-feast. This symbolic meal encouraged growth in God-centered love and the manifestation of spiritual fruit.

Note that in Wesley's hymn the community first invites Jesus as the honored guest of the feast. Jesus comes, and sits, and banquets in the hearts of the faithful. Next, Jesus' table companions pray that the feast might be a "feast of love." Finally, they open their hearts to the inpouring of the Holy Spirit, that they might bear much fruit and become his disciples. What an amazing example of grace!

Pray

True Vine, we glorify you when we bear spiritual fruit: fill us with love, joy, peace, patience, kindness, generosity, faithfulness, gentleness, and self-control, in your Spirit. Amen.

Tenth Day of Christmas

Read

Beloved, let us love one another, because love is from God; everyone who loves is born of God and knows God. Whoever does not love does not know God, for God is love. God's love was revealed among us in this way: God sent his only Son into the world so that we might live through him. . . . We love because he first loved us. Those who say, "I love God," and hate their brothers or sisters, are liars; for those who do not love a brother or sister whom they have seen, cannot love God whom they have not seen. The commandment we have from him is this: those who love God must love their brothers and sisters also. (1 John 4:7–9, 19–21)

Sing

Meter: 88.88.88

This hymn can be sung to Woodbury, one of the traditional settings for the hymn.

> Come, O thou Traveller unknown,
>   Whom still I hold, but cannot see!
> My company before is gone,
>   And I am left alone with thee;
> With thee all night I mean to stay,
> And wrestle till the break of day.
>
> Yield to me now—for I am weak,
>   But confident in self-despair!
> Speak to my heart, in blessings speak,
>   Be conquered by my instant prayer:
> Speak, or thou never hence shalt move,
> And tell me if thy name is LOVE.
>
> 'Tis Love! 'Tis Love! thou diedst for me;
>   I hear thy whisper in my heart.
> The morning breaks, the shadows flee,
>   Pure Universal Love thou art:

> To me, to all, thy mercies move—
> Thy nature, and thy name is LOVE.
> > (*Hymns*, Hymn 136.1, 6–7)

Reflect

Each of us is engaged in the same quest in life. We long for love. We yearn to know that love is real. In a world shaken by terror, violence, and war, and in cultures preoccupied with self, things, and more, we look everywhere for love—the only real thing. Gerhard Tersteegen, the German Pietist and poet, expressed our longings so well in a hymn translated eloquently, not by Charles, but by his brother John:

> Thou hidden love of God, whose height,
> > Whose depth unfathomed, no one knows;
> I see from far thy beauteous light,
> > Inly I sigh for thy repose;
> My heart is pained, nor can it be
> At rest, till it finds rest in thee.
> > (*Hymns*, Hymn 335.1)

Charles Wesley's questions are our questions too. Who is God? Who is Jesus? Can I know God? His discovery can be your discovery as well. In his most profound autobiographical hymn, "Come, O Thou Traveler Unknown," he describes the breakthrough that changed his life—that can change your life. The father of the English hymn, Isaac Watts, claimed that this one hymn was worth all the religious verse he himself had ever penned. In the first seven stanzas of the original hymn, the seeker struggles to know the Unknown Traveler and refuses to let go of the quest "till I thy name, thy nature know." "Tell me if thy name is Love," is the cry of the soul!

Following lengthy struggle, Wesley describes the climactic discovery by means of paradoxical language. Yield to me, because I am weak. Drained of all effort, the exhausted spirit cries out for God to do what only God can do. Confident in self-despair, the weary wrestler prays for a final time: "And tell me if thy name is LOVE."

> 'Tis Love! 'Tis Love! thou diedst for me;
> I hear thy whisper in my heart.

> The morning breaks, the shadows flee,
> Pure Universal Love thou art:
> To me, to all, thy mercies move—
> Thy nature, and thy name is LOVE.

The discovery of faith resounds throughout the remainder of the hymn as a glorious refrain: "Thy nature, and thy name is LOVE." God is Love. Jesus shows us how that love acts in the world. God's nature and name are one and the same: Love! Wesley discovered that God is "pure, universal love" and this discovery became the consistent refrain of his life.

This day celebrates the ten great Laws of God. But of all God's commandments, none supersedes the law of love, revealed and mandated by the incarnate Son of God.

Pray

Loving God, pure, universal Love revealed to us in Jesus: may we, like bounding deer fly home, and prove throughout all eternity that your name and your nature is love. Amen.

ELEVENTH DAY OF CHRISTMAS

Read

[Jesus] is the image of the invisible God, the firstborn of all creation; for in him all things in heaven and on earth were created, things visible and invisible, whether thrones or dominions or rulers or powers—all things have been created through him and for him. He himself is before all things, and in him all things hold together. He is the head of the body, the church; he is the beginning, the firstborn from the dead, so that he might come to have first place in everything. For in him all the fullness of God was pleased to dwell. (Colossians 1:15–19)

Sing

Meter: 88.88.88

This hymn can be sung to St. Petersburg, the tune used for "Before Thy Throne, O God, We Kneel."

Let angels and archangels sing,
　　The wonderful Immanuel's name,
Adore with us our new-born King,
　　And still the joyful news proclaim;
All earth and heaven be ever joined,
To praise the Saviour of mankind.

The everlasting God comes down,
　　To sojourn with the sons of men;
Without his majesty or crown
　　The great Invisible is seen:
Of all his dazzling glories shorn,
The everlasting God is born!

Angels, behold that infant's face,
　　With rapturous awe the Godhead own,
'Tis all your heaven on him to gaze,
　　And cast your crowns before his throne;
Though now he on his footstool lies,
Ye know he built both earth and skies.

By him into existence brought,
　　Ye sang the all-creating word;
Ye heard him call our world from nought;
　　Again, in honour of your Lord,
Ye morning stars, your hymns employ,
And shout, ye sons of God, for joy.

(*Nativity Hymns*, Hymn 13)

Reflect

The incarnation dominates Wesley's lyrical landscape, not only in his hymns on the nativity, but throughout his poetic works. The crucifixion and resurrection of Jesus Christ, of course, complete his redemptive work. These events in human history constitute the central proclamation of the Christian faith. Without this testimony, according to St. Paul, our faith is in vain. But much like the early church fathers, Wesley embraces the notion that here, at the very beginning of God's earthly existence in Jesus, God reveals the great mystery the whole creation has been groaning for in travail until now. The visible person, Jesus Christ, reveals the Invisible God. Wesley encapsulates this central image of the hymn in a simple, but profound, phrase: "Without his majesty or crown The great Invisible is seen."

Christian theologians describe this as the *visio dei*—the vision of God. Note how the Colossians text ponders this mystery of visibility and invisibility: Jesus is "the image of the invisible God." God creates all things—visible and invisible—through and for Christ. In Christ, "the fullness of God was pleased to dwell." In the face of Jesus, the disciples really did see the glory of God! Macarius, an early church father who had a profound influence on the Wesley brothers, observed that, in Christ, God becomes all light and all face and all eye. Perhaps only such mystical language suffices to plumb the depths of this mystery.

Of even greater significance for Charles Wesley, however, is what this actually means for you and me. We need not "go up to heaven" to see God on God's glorious throne. Rather, with Christ, the place of divine abiding—the holy temple or heavenly palace—becomes the Christian soul itself. On this day when we remember the faithful eleven disciples, how glorious to celebrate this eternal fact. Wesley articulates this profound insight in a lyrical paraphrase of Matthew 1:23:

> Fullness of the Deity
> In Jesu's body dwells,
> Dwells in all his saints and me,
> When God his Son reveals:
> Father, manifest thy Son,
> And, conscious of th'incarnate Word,
> In our inmost souls make known
> The presence of the Lord.
>
> (*Ms. Matthew*)

Jesus not only reveals the immortal, invisible, inaccessible God to us, he opens up a space in the human heart—your heart—for this God to dwell. "'Tis all your heaven on him to gaze."

Pray

Invisible God, your Son, Jesus Christ our Lord, reveals you to us fully: dwell in my heart, reveal your presence in my inmost soul, and make me transparent to your love. Amen.

TWELFTH DAY OF CHRISTMAS

Read

For this reason I bow my knees before the Father, from whom every family in heaven and on earth takes its name. I pray that, according to the riches of his glory, he may grant that you may be strengthened in your inner being with power through his Spirit, and that Christ may dwell in your hearts through faith, as you are being rooted and grounded in love. I pray that you may have the power to comprehend, with all the saints, what is the breadth and length and height and depth, and to know the love of Christ that surpasses knowledge, so that you may be filled with all the fullness of God. (Ephesians 3:14–19)

Sing

Meter: 87.87 D

This hymn can be sung to Hyfrydol, the traditional setting for this hymn.

> Love divine, all loves excelling,
>> Joy of heaven, to earth come down,
> Fix in us thy humble dwelling,
>> All thy faithful mercies crown!
> Jesu, thou art all compassion,
>> Pure, unbounded love thou art;
> Visit us with thy salvation!
>> Enter every trembling heart.
>
> Breathe, O breathe thy loving Spirit
>> Into every troubled breast!
> Let us all in thee inherit;
>> Let us find that second rest.

Take away our bent to sinning;
Alpha and Omega be;
End of faith, as its beginning,
Set our hearts at liberty.

Come, almighty to deliver,
Let us all thy grace receive;
Suddenly return, and never,
Never more thy temples leave.
Thee we would be always blessing,
Serve thee as thy hosts above,
Pray, and praise thee without ceasing,
Glory in thy perfect love.

Finish then thy new creation,
Pure and spotless let us be;
Let us see thy great salvation
Perfectly restored in thee;
Changed from glory into glory,
Till in heaven we take our place,
Till we cast our crowns before thee,
Lost in wonder, love, and praise.

(*Hymns*, Hymn 374)

Reflect

We conclude our journey through Advent and the twelve days of Christmas with one of Charles Wesley's most eloquent affirmations of the Christian faith. Like the Apostle's Creed, remembered on this day, Wesley's hymn sums up God's great vision of restored life in Christ. The hymn is a prayer to Jesus as the incarnation of the love of God. He reveals a love that is pure and unbounded, more comprehensive than we ever could have imagined. All creation below and all the saints above adore this Christ, the joy of heaven. We pray in imperative mode: visit us, reside in us, penetrate to the center of our hearts, and dwell with us forever!

The great hymn writer celebrates the effects of the indwelling Spirit of love: she relieves trouble, secures rest, removes the desire to sin, and liberates the hearts of those who put their trust in Christ, the Alpha and Omega. The dominant theme of the Christian life is the desire never to be separated from the unconditional love we have come to know in Jesus; to serve, praise, and glory in this perfect love throughout eternity. The driving impulse of Wesley's vision of the Christian life is the fullest possible restoration of God's image in the life of every believer. Changed from glory into glory, the child of God falls prostrate before the Lord of all creation, "lost in wonder, love, and praise." Wesley's lofty vision to "be filled with all the fullness of God" is nothing other than a poetic paraphrase of the great collect he prayed before receiving the Holy Eucharist in the tradition of The Book of Common Prayer, a prayer I invite you to pray as your final act in this devotional journey.

Pray

Almighty God, unto whom all hearts be open, all desires known, and from whom no secrets are hid; Cleanse the thoughts of our hearts by the inspiration of thy Holy Spirit, that we may perfectly love thee, and worthily magnify thy holy Name; through Christ our Lord. Amen.

PART THREE

Formats for Morning and Evening Prayer

SUGGESTED MORNING PRAYER FORMAT

CALL TO PRAYER
Lord, open our lips.
And our mouth shall proclaim your praise.

Glory to the Father, and to the Son, and to the Holy Spirit: as it was in the beginning, is now, and will be for ever. Amen. Alleluia.

(Throughout the season of Advent)
Our King and Savior now draws near:
Come let us adore him.

(On the Twelve Days of Christmas)
Alleluia. To us a child is born:
Come let us adore him. Alleluia.

PSALM 95:1–7
O come, let us sing to the LORD; let us make a joyful noise to the rock of our salvation! Let us come into his presence with thanksgiving; let us make a joyful noise to him with songs of

praise! For the LORD is a great God, and a great King above all gods. In his hand are the depths of the earth; the heights of the mountains are his also. The sea is his, for he made it, and the dry land, which his hands have formed. O come, let us worship and bow down, let us kneel before the LORD, our Maker! For he is our God, and we are the people of his pasture, and the sheep of his hand. O that today you would listen to his voice!

Glory to the Father, and to the Son, and to the Holy Spirit: as it was in the beginning, is now, and will be for ever. Amen.

SCRIPTURE READING FOR THE DAY

TIME OF REFLECTION

THE TE DEUM

You are God: we praise you;
You are the Lord: we acclaim you;
You are the eternal Father:
All creation worships you.
To you all angels, all the powers of heaven,
Cherubim and Seraphim, sing in endless praise:
    Holy, holy, holy Lord, God of power and might,
    heaven and earth are full of your glory.
The glorious company of apostles praise you.
The noble fellowship of prophets praise you.
The white-robed army of martyrs praise you.
Throughout the world the holy Church acclaims you;
    Father, of majesty unbounded,
    your true and only Son, worthy of all worship,
    and the Holy Spirit, advocate and guide.
You, Christ, are the king of glory,
the eternal Son of the Father.

When you became man to set us free
you did not shun the Virgin's womb.
You overcame the sting of death
and opened the kingdom of heaven to all believers.
You are seated at God's right hand in glory.
We believe that you will come and be our judge.
>Come then, Lord, and help your people,
>bought with the price of your own blood,
>and bring us with your saints
>to glory everlasting.

THE HYMN FOR THE DAY

TIME OF REFLECTION

THE APOSTLES' CREED

I believe in God, the Father almighty,
>creator of heaven and earth.
I believe in Jesus Christ, his only Son, our Lord.
>He was conceived by the power of the Holy Spirit,
>>and born of the Virgin Mary.
>He suffered under Pontius Pilate,
>>was crucified, died, and was buried.
>He descended to the dead.
>On the third day he rose again.
>He ascended into heaven,
>>and is seated at the right hand of the Father.
>He will come again to judge the living and the dead.
I believe in the Holy Spirit,
>the holy catholic Church,
>the communion of saints,
>the forgiveness of sins,
>the resurrection of the body,
>and the life everlasting. Amen.

THE MEDITATION FOR THE DAY

TIME OF REFLECTION

PRAYER

> The Lord be with you.
> **And also with you.**
>
> Lord, have mercy upon us.
> **Christ, have mercy upon us.**
> Lord, have mercy upon us.

THE PRAYER FOR THE DAY

THE LORD'S PRAYER (traditional version)

> **Our Father, who art in heaven,**
> **hallowed be thy Name.**
> **Thy kingdom come,**
> **thy will be done,**
> **on earth as it is in heaven.**
> **Give us this day our daily bread.**
> **And forgive us our trespasses,**
> **as we forgive those**
> **who trespass against us.**
> **And lead us not into temptation,**
> **but deliver us from evil.**
> **For thine is the kingdom,**
> **and the power, and the glory,**
> **for ever and ever. Amen.**

THE MORNING COLLECTS

Lord God, almighty and everlasting Father, you have brought us in safety to this new day: Preserve us with your mighty power, that we do not fall into sin, nor be overcome by adversity; and in all we do, direct us to the fulfilling of your purpose; through Jesus Christ our Lord. Amen.

Almighty God, you have given us grace at this time with one accord to make our common supplication to you; and you have promised through your well-beloved Son that when two or three are gathered together in his Name you will be in the midst of them: Fulfill now, O Lord, our desires and petitions as may be best for us; granting us in this world knowledge of your truth, and in the age to come life everlasting. Amen.

The grace of our Lord Jesus Christ, and the love of God, and the fellowship of the Holy Spirit, be with us all evermore. Amen.

SUGGESTED EVENING PRAYER FORMAT

CALL TO PRAYER

O God, make speed to save us.
O Lord, make haste to help us.

Glory to the Father, and to the Son, and to the Holy Spirit: as it was in the beginning, is now, and will be for ever. Amen. Alleluia.

(Throughout the season of Advent)
Our King and Savior now draws near:
Come let us adore him.

(On the Twelve Days of Christmas)
Alleluia. To us a child is born:
Come let us adore him. Alleluia.

PSALM 98

O sing to the LORD a new song, for he has done marvelous things. His right hand and his holy arm have gotten him victory. The LORD has made known his victory; he has revealed his vindication in the sight of the nations. He has remembered his steadfast love and faithfulness to the house of Israel. All the ends of the earth have seen the victory of our God. Make a joyful noise to the LORD, all the earth; break forth into joyous song and sing praises. Sing praises to the LORD with the lyre, with the lyre and the sound of melody. With trumpets and the sound of the horn make a joyful noise before the King, the LORD. Let the sea roar, and all that fills it; the world and those who live in it. Let the floods clap their hands; let the hills sing together for joy at the presence of the LORD, for he is coming to judge the earth. He will judge the world with righteousness, and the peoples with equity.

Glory to the Father, and to the Son, and to the Holy Spirit: as it was in the beginning, is now, and will be for ever. Amen.

SCRIPTURE READING FOR THE DAY

TIME OF REFLECTION

THE MAGNIFICAT

My soul magnifies the Lord,
　　　and my spirit rejoices in God my Savior,
　　　for he has looked with favor
　　　on the lowliness of his servant.
Surely, from now on all generations will call me blessed;
　　　for the Mighty One has done great things for me,
　　　and holy is his name.
　　　His mercy is for those who fear him

from generation to generation.
He has shown strength with his arm;
    he has scattered the proud in the thoughts of their hearts.
He has brought down the powerful from their thrones,
    and lifted up the lowly;
    he has filled the hungry with good things,
    and sent the rich away empty.
He has helped his servant Israel,
    in remembrance of his mercy,
    according to the promise he made to our ancestors,
    to Abraham and to his descendants forever.

THE HYMN FOR THE DAY

TIME OF REFLECTION

THE APOSTLES' CREED

I believe in God, the Father almighty,
    creator of heaven and earth.
I believe in Jesus Christ, his only Son, our Lord.
    He was conceived by the power of the Holy Spirit,
        and born of the Virgin Mary.
    He suffered under Pontius Pilate,
        was crucified, died, and was buried.
    He descended to the dead.
    On the third day he rose again.
    He ascended into heaven,
        and is seated at the right hand of the Father.
    He will come again to judge the living and the dead.
I believe in the Holy Spirit,
    the holy catholic Church,
    the communion of saints,
    the forgiveness of sins,
    the resurrection of the body,
    and the life everlasting. Amen.

THE SONG OF SIMEON (*Nunc dimittis*)

**Lord, you now have set your servant free
    to go in peace as you have promised;
For these eyes of mine have seen the Savior,
    whom you have prepared for all the world to see:
A Light to enlighten the nations,
    and the glory of your people Israel.**

**Glory to the Father, and to the Son, and to the Holy Spirit: as
it was in the beginning, is now, and will be for ever. Amen.**

THE MEDITATION FOR THE DAY

TIME OF REFLECTION

PRAYER

The Lord be with you.
And also with you.

Lord, have mercy upon us.
Christ, have mercy upon us.
Lord, have mercy upon us.

THE PRAYER FOR THE DAY

THE LORD'S PRAYER (traditional version)

**Our Father, who art in heaven,
    hallowed be thy Name.
thy kingdom come,**

thy will be done,
  on earth as it is in heaven.
Give us this day our daily bread.
And forgive us our trespasses,
as we forgive those
  who trespass against us.
And lead us not into temptation,
  but deliver us from evil.
For thine is the kingdom,
  and the power, and the glory,
  for ever and ever. Amen.

THE EVENING COLLECTS (traditional versions)

Most holy God, the source of all good desires, all right judgments, and all just works: Give to us, your servants, that peace which the world cannot give, so that our minds may be fixed on the doing of your will, and that we, being delivered from the fear of all enemies, may live in peace and quietness; through the mercies of Christ Jesus our Savior. Amen.

Almighty God, you have given us grace at this time with one accord to make our common supplication to you; and you have promised through your well-beloved Son that when two or three are gathered together in his Name you will be in the midst of them: Fulfill now, O Lord, our desires and petitions as may be best for us; granting us in this world knowledge of your truth, and in the age to come life everlasting. Amen.

The grace of our Lord Jesus Christ, and the love of God, and the fellowship of the Holy Spirit, be with us all evermore. Amen.

Hymn Sources

Short Titles and Abbreviations for
Poetry/Hymn Publications
by John and/or Charles Wesley

Family Hymns	*Hymns for the Use of Families, and on various Occasions* (Bristol: Pine, 1767).
HLS	*Hymns on the Lord's Supper* (Bristol: Farley, 1745).
HSP (1739)	*Hymns and Sacred Poems* (London: Strahan, 1739).
HSP (1740)	*Hymns and Sacred Poems* (London: Strahan, 1740).
HSP (1749)	*Hymns and Sacred Poems*, 2 vols. (Bristol: Farley, 1749).
Hymns	*A Collection of Hymns for the use of the People Called Methodists* (London: Paramore, 1780).
Ms. Matthew	*Manuscript Poems on the Gospel of St. Matthew*

Nativity Hymns	*Hymns for the Nativity of our Lord* (London: Strahan, 1745).
Preacher Hymns	*Hymns for the Use of Methodist Preachers* (n.p., 1760).
Redemption Hymns	*Hymns for those that see, and those that have Redemption in the Blood of Jesus Christ* (London: Strahan, 1747).
Scripture Hymns	*Short Hymns on Select Passages of the Holy Scriptures*, 2 vols. (Bristol: Farley, 1762).
Unpublished Hymns	*The Unpublished Poetry of Charles Wesley,* edited by S T Kimbrough, Jr. and Oliver A. Beckerlegge, 3 vols. (Nashville: Kingswood Books, 1988–1992).

Scripture Index

Hymn Tune and Meter Index

Rockingham (LM)	Advent 3 Saturday	47
St. Agnes (CM)	Advent 3 Thursday	42
St. Catherine (88.88.88)	Advent 1 Friday	12
St. George's Windsor (77.77 D)	Christmas 9	87
St. Petersburg (88.88.88)	Christmas 11	91–92
Savannah (77.77)	Christmas 7	82
Stuttgart (87.87)	Advent 1 Sunday	1
Surrey (88.88.88)	St. Stephen	70
Tallis' Canon (LM)	Advent 4 Sunday	49
The Call (77.77)	Advent 1 Wednesday	8
Unusual Meter (555 11)	Advent 1 Saturday	14
Unusual Meter (55 11)	Christmas 5	76
Unusual Meter (665 11)	Advent 1 Monday	3
Unusual Meter (66.77.77)	Advent 4 Friday	61
Unusual Meter (76.76.88.76)	Advent 4 Monday	51
Unusual Meter (77.44.7)	Advent 4 Thursday	58
Unusual Meter (8.33.6)	Advent 3 Wednesday	39
Unusual Meter (886 D)	Advent 2 Thursday;	26
	Advent 3 Tuesday;	37
	Advent 3 Friday;	44
	Christmas;	68
	Holy Name	
Vater unser im Himmelreich (88.88.88)	Christmas 8	84
Winchester Old (CM)	Advent 1 Tuesday	5
Woodbury (88.88.88)	Christmas 10	89

Note: Some 888.888 times may substitute appropriately in the unusual 886D meter.